T3-BNW-604

ALA Studies in Librarianship
Number 4

Guide
to the Development
of Educational Media
Selection
Centers

CORA PAUL BOMAR
Program Director

M. Ann Heidbreder and
Carol A. Nemeyer
Program Coordinators

AMERICAN LIBRARY ASSOCIATION
Chicago

Library of Congress Cataloging in Publication Data

Bomar, Cora Paul, 1913–
  Guide to the development of educational media
selection centers.

  (ALA studies in librarianship, no. 4)
  Report on phase 2 of the Educational Media Selection
Centers Program.
  Report on phase 1, edited by J. Rowell and M. A.
Heidbreder, published in 1971 under title: Educational
media selection centers.
  Bibliography: p.
  1. Instructional materials centers. I. Heidbreder,
M. Ann, joint author. II. Nemeyer, Carol A., 1929–
joint author. III. Title. IV. Series: American
Library Association. ALA studies in librarianship, no. 4.

LB3044.B65   021'.2   73-3362
ISBN 0-8389-0123-9

The research reported herein was performed pursuant to a contract with the Office of Education, U.S. Department of Health, Education, and Welfare. Contractors undertaking such projects under government sponsorship are encouraged to express freely their professional judgment in the conduct of the project. Points of view or opinions stated do not, therefore, necessarily represent official Office of Education position or policy.

The final report for the Educational Media Selection Centers Project, Phase II, was submitted by the National Book Committee to the Office of Education under the title THE ORGANIZATION AND OPERATION OF EDUCATIONAL MEDIA SELECTION CENTERS: Guide to the Development of Educational Media Selection Centers. The Project Number is OEC-0-8-08515-4438 (095).

Printed in the United States of America

Third printing, March 1976

Contents

iii

List of Contributors
and Topics

ELENORA ALEXANDER
    Director of Instructional Materials
    Services
    Houston Independent School
    District

COLLECTIONS

RICHARD L. DARLING
    Dean, School of Library Service
    Columbia University

RESEARCH

ALEXANDER FRAZIER
    College of Education
    The Ohio State University

RATIONALE FOR THE EMSC

MAE GRAHAM
    Assistant Director, Division of
    Library Development and Services
    Maryland State Department of
    Education

BUDGET

M. ANN HEIDBREDER
    Director of Library Services
    Harcourt Brace Jovanovich, Inc.

EMSC: SCOPE AND
    BACKGROUND

LORE HOWARD
    Chief, Bureau of School Libraries
    The University of the State of New
    York
    The State Education Department

FACILITIES

MARVIN R. A. JOHNSON
    Consulting Architect
    Division of School Planning
    North Carolina Department of
    Public Instruction

FACILITIES

MARY FRANCES K. JOHNSON
  Associate Professor
  School of Education
  University of North Carolina
  at Greensboro

PROGRAM

VIRGINIA MCJENKIN
  Formerly Director, School Libraries
  Fulton County (Georgia) Board
  of Education

INSERVICE EDUCATION
AND TRAINING

SARAH JONES
  Formerly Supervisor, School
  Libraries
  Georgia Department of Education

INSERVICE EDUCATION
AND TRAINING

RUSSELL SHANK
  Director of Libraries
  Smithsonian Institution

NETWORKS

SARA SRYGLEY
  Professor
  School of Library Science
  The Florida State University

ADMINISTRATIVE STRUCTURES

PEGGY SULLIVAN
  Assistant Professor
  Graduate School of Library and
  Information Science
  University of Pittsburgh

STAFF

RALPH WILEMAN
  Associate Professor
  School of Education
  University of North Carolina
  at Chapel Hill

EVALUATION

Preface

In 1968, when the National Book Committee launched the first comprehensive study of educational media selection centers, the basic question was, "What is being done, and what more should be done, to assure the maximum effective utilization of educational media in any instructional setting or learning environment?"

The question was deceptively simple. It became almost immediately evident that the concept included complex and sensitive problems in defining behavioral objectives within a context of existing educational technology. Further, it was recognized that the learning process is continuous throughout a lifetime and that educational goals are established to a significant extent by each learner.

We live today in an all-media culture. While people are often stimulated to learn without an array of media at hand, the motivation and capacity to continue and to enjoy learning cannot usually be sustained by one medium of communication. We need access to the necessary book, film, tape, photograph, periodical, map, and other traditional and newer media. During the past five years, patterns of teacher-directed instruction have been modified to accommodate individualized forms of learning. One need only browse through current media catalogs to realize that the amount of learning resources is constantly burgeoning. Continuing innovations in both formal and informal educational enterprises require new and flexible means to help both students and teachers in the evaluation, selection, and effective use of educational media.

Educational media selection centers are not the single answer, but used effectively in conjunction with existing libraries, schools, civic centers and the like, an interactive system of media centers would greatly advance progress toward educational goals. Most remaining problems created by an unhealthy and unrealistic dichotomy of print and nonprint media are approaching solution. The present report proceeds on the assumption that all kinds of media are important; all are incorporated into the EMSC concept. In reporting the second phase of the EMSC Program, an effort is made to avoid duplicating many of the details supporting the significant findings recorded in the Phase I report: *Educational Media Selection Centers:* Identification and Analysis of Current Practices, published by ALA in 1971. The reader is urged to refer to this work to gain useful background for the present report.

The GUIDE is not intended as a blueprint for establishing uniform media centers, nor should it be construed as a set of standards. The ideas and data offered here should, however, stimulate creative thinking about ways to improve existing centers and begin new ones. A group of experts share their best professional judgment in this discussion about how educational media selection centers can be organized, staffed, administered, and equipped. These experts also suggest how EMSCs can be used to evaluate media and to distribute evaluations widely. They talk about the importance of inservice education and tell how centers work individually and as components of local, regional, state and national networks.

The GUIDE thus represents the thinking and effort of many persons. It speaks to anyone and all who wish to begin or to change a center's program at the local, district, or state level. And the GUIDE looks to a future national network of centers—perhaps its most far-reaching, innovative message.

CORA PAUL BOMAR
Program Director

Acknowledgments

We are extremely grateful to all the contributors whose words and concepts are blended into this report and to the many people in the field who have offered their help and shown great interest in the program. We wish to thank Paul Janaske and Henry Drennan of the U.S. Office of Education for administering the OE grant for this study; they kept red tape to a minimum and offered wise counsel.

Two of the most indefatigable professional library leaders contributed immensely to the EMSC Program: Mary Virginia Gaver and Frances Henne. Each has served well beyond the call, reading early drafts of the report and offering advice generously. Thanks are given to the many persons who serve or have served as advisers to the program, as listed in the first appendix.

A project this complex needs direction and coordination. Cora Paul Bomar, Program Director of Phase II, has again shown administrative acumen and ability to draw excellent people into the program and keep them involved. M. Ann Heidbreder's expertness and understanding of the evaluation of media and of the publishing industry have been doubly tapped, first as Coordinator and currently as an active member of the EMSC Executive Advisory Committee. In 1971 Carol A. Nemeyer was assigned to the program as Phase II Coordinator. She has had the task of gathering and analyzing the content of this GUIDE and, with Peter Jennison's editorial help, developed this final report.

In short, my deepest thanks to all.

JOHN C. FRANTZ
Executive Director
National Book Committee, Inc.

ix

1

Introduction
to the EMSC Program

The Educational Media Selection Centers Program was begun in 1968 in response to growing concern about the quality of the evaluation of media being carried out in the United States and about the effective use of media with learners of all ages.

The quantity of media of all kinds—print and nonprint—published and produced for educational and general markets had grown rapidly in the last 15 years. In 1955, 12,500 books were published; by 1967 the number of titles in book format alone had grown to 28,700. Educators, parents, librarians, and publishers were all aware that the task of evaluating materials had become extraordinarily complex and time-consuming. They realized, too, that many books and other materials were being evaluated and selected in isolation from other available media: e.g., books were being handled in one manner and audiovisual and other nonprint materials such as models and games, in another, with different criteria applied. The need for a coordinated approach to the task became apparent if children and their teachers were to receive maximum benefit from materials and from programs to encourage their use in schools and libraries.

At the same time, it became more and more evident that major changes needed to be made in the education of teachers, especially in the evaluation of media and their use with students.

Inservice education programs help to meet this need, as do summer courses in colleges and universities, workshops, and institutes. However, the greatest number of classroom teachers, administrators, curriculum coordinators, media specialists, librarians, and other educators can be reached during the school year where they are living and working. Such programs would allow them to attend sessions at convenient times, to try out materials in the classroom during the evaluation period, to meet and talk with professionals who can give them immediate, specific advice, and to select the materials they need to achieve their goals.

All of these factors motivated the National Book Committee, a nonprofit association of citizens, to prepare and submit a proposal for a four-phase

1

project, of which two phases have been funded by the U.S. Office of Education. USOE was especially interested in the concept of educational media selection centers for several reasons. Many school systems were submitting proposals to establish centers of one kind or another to collect, evaluate, or produce media (especially the newer media) or to upgrade the quality of their teacher education programs, in cooperation with colleges and universities. Other proposals emerged for "systems" to handle the evaluation and recording of evaluations of media. The Office of Education was therefore receptive to a proposal for active study in this general area. Such a project as the EMSC Program seemed especially appropriate for the federal government to fund since it has invested so much money in curriculum research in general, in the development of newer media, and in the better use of existing media in particular. If it is true that the quality of education is improved when the quality of materials used with students is improved, then it is also true that materials need to be evaluated according to valid, high standards so that the most effective tools are given to teachers and other educators to do the best job possible.

To provide expert guidance for the project, the National Book Committee invited leaders in the education, library, and information science fields to serve on the Executive Advisory Council, chaired by Mason W. Gross, then president of Rutgers, the State University of New Jersey. To assure an even wider range of professional guidance for the completion of Phase I and to help plan and implement the subsequent phases of the program, a representational Advisory Committee of more than fifty national education and library organizations was formed. (Members of both groups are given in appendix 1.) The Advisory Committee, which has absorbed the original Executive Advisory Council, with Dr. Gross continuing as chairman of the expanded group, held its first meeting in the fall of 1969. The Phase I report, which includes full details of the research methodology employed, was written by the staff, criticized and improved by various members of the Advisory Committee, and submitted to USOE on January 30, 1970.[1] The Phase I recommendation that could be implemented immediately was that work go forward on Phase II, devoted to the preparation of a guide to the development of educational media selection centers.

One point must be kept in mind by the reader. This GUIDE is just that. It is *not* a set of standards. It is a document intended to assist the work of those who want to establish and improve educational media selection centers. Portions of it will probably be implemented in the model/demon-

---

[1] In Phase I two questionnaires were mailed—the first to all known facilities, the second to 440 identified centers. On the basis of the findings, 38 centers were selected for on-site evaluation by professional research teams. Their reports were analyzed and tabulated, and, when feasible, team members later participated in group discussion sessions.

2

stration phase of the EMSC Program, but the GUIDE is intended as more than a blueprint for any model program.

The first step in Phase I was to find out what kinds of media evaluation were being done in the country and where. This phase of the EMSC Program, a location/identification study, was completed in January 1970, and the report, *Educational Media Selection Centers,* was published in 1971 by the American Library Association. The major findings of the study were that few, if any, educational media selection centers existed which fulfilled the definition set forth by the EMSC Program:

> Ideally, such a center is a place which houses a wide variety of media and which conducts a full-scale training program in the techniques of selecting and using media for librarians, teachers, educational supervisory personnel, and other adults. The media in these centers are professionally evaluated and purchased. Various other services (in-service guidance, dynamics of utilization of media in schools, identification of sources of materials and procedures for acquisition) are offered.[2]

Several facilities in the nation evaluate some media, but not one of them covered all potentially useful items or all forms of educational media in a highly professional manner. Furthermore, very few helped to educate adults in the use of media. In some places the program was fragmented; in others the collections segregated by kinds of media, age level, subject matter, or other category. The second major finding was a deep interest among educators, librarians, publishers and producers, administrators and other involved personnel in an improved approach to the entire problem of evaluating materials and using them most effectively with children, young people, and adults who need remedial instruction.

Because there is such evident need for effective educational media selection centers, Phase II of the program was devoted to the preparation of this guide to their development. A team of twenty-five experts in various areas was asked to contribute. Some met with the staff to give advice about gathering information; others wrote portions of chapters or entire chapters. Because so few centers existed which could be studied, visited, analyzed, and otherwise presented for general consideration, the contributors were asked to share their best professional opinions and judgments about all facets of their subject. An Executive Committee of the EMSC Advisory Committee (listed in appendix 1) serves as the operational group of advisers for Phase II. The EMSC staff interviewed many professionals and

[2] John Rowell and M. Ann Heidbreder, *Educational Media Selection Centers: Identification and Analysis of Current Practices* (Chicago: American Library Assn., 1971), p.1–2.

assembled their ideas into this document. Its intended audiences are educators—including administrators, librarians, and media specialists—and other adults working with children and youth, persons responsible for the use of media in all kinds of programs. This guide should help those who want to establish centers or redirect or expand existing programs. Although it was not possible to provide specific information on every aspect of the subject (especially in the area of budgeting), the information in this guide should be immediately useful to anyone who wishes to launch or change a selection center or program at the local level. Work can begin now—without a computer, or a new kind of staff, or a brand-new building, or an entirely new system for evaluating and acquiring materials. It is strongly recommended that local selection centers and evaluation programs be supported and improved. It is essential that effective grass roots efforts continue and that these experiences be shared.

Assuming funding of Phase III of the program, model or demonstration centers will be opened across the country so that the policies and procedures set forth here can be tested. Optimum existing programs can be brought into Phase III, although it is recommended that at least one model center be started anew. Desirably, the centers should be located in a variety of administrative and geographic situations, serving urban and rural youth, so that the widest possible sample of experience and exposure can be assured.

The importance of the EMSC Program has been proved in many ways, but several significant points should be recorded here:

1. When one looks at the tremendous changes being made in the process of education in this country today, the importance of effective use of instructional materials cannot be doubted. Decentralization of major school systems and other educational institutions and increased individualizing of instruction at all levels point toward the greater involvement of classroom teachers and students themselves in the evaluation and use of media.

Students today are exposed earlier to many different kinds of experiences —actual and vicarious—than they were even fifteen years ago. They develop interests in more complicated and sophisticated subjects at an earlier age than they did in the past. *Current* events are just that: young people want to explore—to learn more about what they hear *when* they hear it. Information is coming to them from a great variety of sources. Television and radio are with them from the day they are born. Schools, libraries, bookstores, music stores, movie theaters, department and drug stores are filled with materials to read, listen to, watch, and touch. Students use tapes and other recordings in schools and buy them for home listening. Thus they communicate more comfortably with and through all media than did students in the 1950s or even in the 1960s; and they expect high-quality educational materials.

4

2. Few people would question the need for professional evaluation of media, or the relationship between quality evaluation and purchase and the eventual upgrading of what is published and produced for evaluation and purchase. As long as an inferior product is bought, it will be produced; when it cannot be sold, the producer begins to wonder why, which can lead to product improvement.

There are significant limitations to the evaluation functions which can appropriately be assigned to the kinds of centers referred to throughout this guide. For example, the centers are not designed, even as part of a network, to deal with very large, comprehensive instructional systems. Some complex multimedia learning systems are intended for basal adoption (i.e., those constituting the basic system for teaching reading for an entire school system) and cannot be evaluated effectively until they have had extended use in real situations. Nor can any individual component of such a learning system be evaluated per se. What a center can do, however, is collect and disseminate valid evaluations which have been made of such basic systems.

There are strong, sometimes divergent, opinions about ways in which the evaluation of media should be made and by whom. Some educators believe that the various forms of media should be evaluated separately—books and other printed materials by teachers and librarians, and audiovisual materials by audiovisual specialists. Although the actual evaluation should, of course, be accomplished by the most proficient professionals, the total evaluation program should be a coordinated effort so that the learner, his needs, and the curriculum in which the materials are to be used determine the criteria for evaluation. If media are selected in isolation, they tend to be used that way. Thus teachers and students do not have access to the full range of items available to them. The EMSC Program has helped to point out the problems inherent in evaluation programs that treat print and nonprint media separately, as was fully documented during Phase I and in the writing of the Phase II report. Centers such as those envisioned in Phase III would do a great deal to break down the practice of separate evaluation and selection, by bringing all kinds of appropriate media together in one place and by encouraging their coordinated use. In the words of the Phase I report:

> The future success of educational media selection centers will require strong directors who embrace both print and audiovisual concepts. Centers that are represented by two different people, i.e., print and nonprint, or centers whose directors heavily lean toward one of the two lines of media are likely to have difficulties.[3]

3 Ibid., p.81.

3. The pressing need for improved education in the evaluation and use of media in schools, and for conferences, institutes, and workshops is repeatedly expressed. Few institutions are prepared to offer what they consider adequate programs in media for today's teachers and librarians. Some immediate needs have been met through summer sessions, institutes, and workshops under the National Defense Education Act (NDEA) and the Higher Education Act (HEA), and programs of professional associations, special courses, and inservice programs in local school and library systems and at the state level. However, the strong impression remains that great numbers of college graduates are entering the teaching fields ill prepared to evaluate materials professionally and with little experience in using media with students.

The educational component of the EMSC Program is, therefore, extremely important. The kind of instructional programs conducted in and by a center, the ways in which a center promotes its service to a user, and the degree of feedback the center seeks and gets from its users can make or break the center—indeed, the entire concept of an EMSC.

4. Those involved in the EMSC Program and in publishing and producing media, teachers, and other concerned adults recognize the need for hard, comprehensive and current research in the effects of reading, listening, and watching on students and their performance in schools. The needed research falls into two general categories:

a. Research in the general area of media evaluation and use (how materials are evaluated, selected, and field tested; how various items are related one to the other by good teachers and librarians; how deeply *can* students be involved in the evaluation of materials; what *happens* when books, films, filmstrips, records, and other items are used effectively in particular situations)

b. A planned research effort for the EMSC Program (what differences does an EMSC make in the general quality of education; what kinds of educational programs appeal to which teachers; in what manner should the EMSC respond to various instructional and learning modes and needs).

Some of this research should be generated and conducted in the centers that come into Phase III of the program. Some of it should be planned by school librarians and other media specialists and conducted through their professional organizations and school groups. Further research should be proposed to the federal government to be carried out in conjunction with regional education laboratories, research and development centers, and other established groups working at the national level. The primary weaknesses of past efforts in this area are that the research studies have been fragmentary or too narrow to be generally applicable or that the groups of students have been too small. The EMSC Program can offer a coordinating office for this needed research and help to recruit and prepare personnel to work in the field.

The complexity and magnitude of the problem of media evaluation and use can cause educators and other concerned adults to lose sight of the ultimate beneficiary—the learner or student. Ultimately this person is the object of the educational enterprise, in the largest sense of the term, and the benefits to the individual must be kept clearly in mind as all the other steps are taken. Although students themselves do not use the center, these places and the overall EMSC concept exist to upgrade the quality of education being offered.

POLICIES AND PROCEDURES OF THE PROGRAM

The EMSC Program deals with a concept which is new to many educators, administrators, and librarians and which needs constant explanation and interpretation. In the EMSC Program the word *media* means published or produced materials that are appropriate for educational use in the broadest sense, not only in formal classroom courses. In the past the textbook was the primary, and often the sole, teaching tool; today it is supplemented by a wide variety of media, in many kinds of formats. Among such media are general books, periodicals, documents, pamphlets, photographs, reproductions, pictorial or graphic works, musical scores, maps, charts, globes, sound recordings, slides, transparencies, films, filmstrips, kinescopes, and videotapes. Yet not all teachers and students are benefiting from the various high quality educational media available. Children are being taught how to read (though not with universal effectiveness), but too few educational systems are offering children a real range of materials to read after they have mastered the basic skills. Similarly, the visual, auditory, and tactile learning media have not been exploited to an extent commensurate with their educational importance and potential, largely because those who are in a position to select, purchase, and use media rarely have access to a comprehensive, current collection for examination and comparison.

A partial and effective solution to this last problem lies in professionally conducted, community-based training programs for inservice teachers, librarians, media specialists, curriculum supervisors, and other adults (both inside and out of the formal school system). A wide variety and number of appropriate media must support such instruction. The inservice trainee must be able to examine and evaluate available media before attempting to

7

use them. Such instruction comprises the major portion of the program (instructional function) of an educational media selection center. Thus, the function and responsibility of the center are conceived to be: (1) a comprehensive collection of teaching and learning media which serves as a depository for examination and selection, and (2) a place where inservice education programs in the selection and use of these resources are conducted.

Traditionally, librarians and media specialists have been responsible for the evaluation and selection of all types of materials, and are now assuming an increasing responsibility for instructing teachers and other adults to use media with students. This instructional leadership is, however, handicapped by a shortage of qualified manpower. Given the quantity and range of existing material, coupled with a critical shortage of trained specialists, it will be virtually impossible in the foreseeable future to staff individual schools with highly skilled specialists. Therefore, it is essential that a coordinated effort be made now to establish centralized resources, where highly skilled media specialists can maximize their effectiveness.

The existence of such educational media selection centers should have a substantive effect on the quality of education for all students, but especially so for the educationally disadvantaged. Many teachers and other professionals are unaware of the existence of media that would help them reach and motivate these children, particularly at the preschool and primary levels.

Where it has often been impractical for teachers to be released from their classrooms for extended periods of time for prolonged inservice instruction or other advanced professional courses, the media selection center can offer convenient and immediate help with specific problems. Full and frequent use of the center's program and resources could provide another avenue toward continuing professional development and help to stimulate new ideas and techniques.

During the course of the first phase of the EMSC Program, the concept of the educational media selection center was transformed from one of a depository to that of a service. Repeatedly, participants in the project expressed a readiness to learn from one another in the process of discovering; this attitude was reflected in reports of the constant growth and change in concepts and definitions of progress, service, and administrative techniques in the centers themselves. Begun as an information-gathering study, Phase I of the project became a catalyst for action within the centers. The objectives for Phase I were:

To establish advisory and administrative operations for the project
To develop data-gathering instruments that would identify existing educational media selection centers in the United States

8

To evaluate the centers so identified and to select those centers or programs which, in one or more aspects, were performing at a level justifying further research

To develop a second, more comprehensive, questionnaire with which to study those centers or programs selected after interpreting the initial data, identifying components of strengths and weaknesses of these centers as related to their operation and effectiveness

To direct on-site team visits to a sampling of centers selected from evaluation of the data from the two questionnaires

To gather information from the on-site visiting teams for the final report on Phase I, preparatory to the development and drafting of the "Guide to the Development of Educational Media Selection Centers" (Phase II).

_____ **2**

Why Centers Are Needed

Setting up evening and Saturday classes in African culture is one of the projects newly authorized by a Model Cities council. The lay committee and its staff are seeking help in developing or expanding a purchase list of useful books, pictures, and filmstrips. Where do they go for assistance in the selection of such materials?

New emphasis on environmental education in elementary schools has just been announced by a midwestern State Department of Public Instruction. Where can a committee of teachers from a local school go to examine media to be added to what is already on hand?

A remedial "Right to Read" project for children in inner-city schools has been undertaken by a group of volunteers assembled by the Junior League of a good-sized city in the East. Who can help them find the books that have proved most exciting and useful in this kind of program, and to locate films that might stimulate further interest in the field opened up by interest in a particular book? Or, where might the person in charge of the program find a filmstrip to help instruct the volunteer?

Sex education materials for use with suburban teenagers are being sought by a Sunday school staff composed of lay persons. Who can help?

Questions like these arise every day in communities of all sizes across the country, where the identification and evaluation of new media is urgent. Local public and school librarians can and do answer such questions. Specialists in audiovisual media assigned to schools and libraries can and do help; indeed, their work will be reinforced by media centers and the centers will depend upon evaluations made by these professionals. But few teachers, librarians, and other media specialists can reasonably be expected to recognize more than the peak of the iceberg or to identify the full spectrum of material available. The crux of the matter is how to get total coverage, especially in a period of school decentralization, reorganization of systems to achieve integration, and radical reform in the learning process. These changes involve increasing reliance on a far greater

10

variety of materials. Public and school librarians and media specialists clearly see the need for and seek opportunities to upgrade and maintain their competencies in order to respond to local demands.

The urgency of widespread need calls for a combination of resources and services not presently found in many places. Today's adult users of educational media with children require and demand sources for the systematic review and evaluation of media. They increasingly need opportunities to develop the skills for effective utilization of the media in specialized learning situations.

The development of Educational Media Selection Centers promises to provide such help. The rationale for Center development includes these significant factors: (1) rapid proliferation in the numbers and variety of educational media, and heightened appreciation of their use; (2) new demands of changing school curricula; and (3) broader community involvement in educational programs in and out of schools.

THE PROLIFERATION AND APPRECIATION
OF VARIED MEDIA

Modern man has had to learn to live with an often almost overwhelming new wealth of information. The target of a ceaseless onslaught of multisensory stimuli, man also learns to screen out much that demands his attention.

But in the process of becoming necessarily more selective in a highly commercialized culture, the modern consumer (as receptor) is learning to value what he chooses by turning from one to another medium. On the way home he may pick up the 5 o'clock radio newscast. Later, as he scans the newspaper, he checks for more details on major events. Then he watches the 6:30 televised reports from Washington, New York, Miami, Houston, and London to confirm and perhaps expand what he already knows. Each of these sources may cover the same events, but the kind of data each has to offer varies greatly. The information consumer thus comes to depend upon the media mixture for the whole picture.

Screening-out is one response of overstimulated eye- and ear-saturated senses—in an environment that attempts to exploit the passivity of the audience. But weeding-out is another response to situations where more information is wanted and where the educated eye and ear have come to recognize and value what each medium has to offer. In either case, the principle is one of selectivity.

Growing appreciation of what each medium has to offer and how media may best be combined provides one of the major reasons for creating educational media selection centers. The user's developing sense of how the uniqueness of each medium can contribute to greater effectiveness in instruction is first sharpened; second, and consequently, the plurality of media as a good in itself is stressed.

A center should concern itself with the nature and contribution of each medium. Users' more-or-less unconscious appreciation of what a good combination of media offers is conditioned by their experience as receptors. But the true uniqueness of media and the necessary interrelatedness has not been made fully explicit, as it needs to be if choices are to match specific needs. What a map can do that a running text cannot may need to be demonstrated even to persons well versed in the use of both.

Why should there be less awareness of the uniqueness of media at the conscious level than at the unexamined level of practice? Part of the answer is that, historically, print has been more familiar. Other media have usually been seen as subordinate to print. Woodcuts and engravings were first used in books as illustrations of the text, dependent upon it and valuable primarily in relationship to it. That many kinds of data not possible to present adequately in words could be presented easily in pictures and diagrams was not well understood at first, and is still not entirely accepted at the conscious level. Even today the first response to a book amply provided with photographs and other graphics is often thumbing through "to look at pictures."

Other remnants of the lack of understanding of the uniqueness of media are also easily identifiable. In the older vocabulary of audiovisual education, for example, slides, flat pictures, models, and the like were referred to as "aids" to teaching or as "supplementary" materials of instruction. Such devices were used *after* a topic had been studied in the book. Today, many, perhaps most, curriculum guides or course outlines are still built around reading, although the assignments may involve several books rather than one. Last to be listed, more often than not, are the audiovisual resources likely to be useful for enrichment—if or as time permits.

Even advocates of multiple media in teaching sometimes still promote the use of films or tapes because of the "difference in interest level" or the need for "a change of pace." If children get bored reading, give them audiovisual exposure as relief, just as they should have a balance between passive and active learning, individual and group activity, or indoor and outdoor pursuits.

Some educators have more recently been suggesting that children who cannot absorb information from books may simply be revealing a difference in learning style. Audiovisual media may be easier for them to learn from than books. This proposition ignores the extent to which instruction is still print bound, and thus why the very young learner is kept from learning much of anything else until (or unless) he learns to read. But the notion that nonprint media are alternatives to print reveals a basic lack of insight into media uniquenesses.

One of the principal needs of adult users of educational media is help in becoming fully alert to the value of a particular medium. An educational media selection center helps meet this need for its clients and continues to serve them in examining and evaluating new media as they are developed and marketed. Almost invariably a new medium is exploited early in its history by persons not fully aware of what it can do that other media cannot. When films were added to the educational mix, for example, almost as many frames were devoted to printed explanations as to motion pictures or animation. As sound was added, the commentary often tried to compete with the textbook. The educational use of television is still hampered by lack of appreciation for what that medium can do that a standup teacher, even when supplied with the widest possible array of flip charts, cannot.

The demand for help by regular clients of such centers will also be increased as more elaborate multimedia programs and installations come on the market.

NEW DEMANDS IN SCHOOL CURRICULA

American society has always made extraordinary cultural demands on its schools, from colonial days and the propagation of the Puritan ethic, to the era of post-Sputnik competition with the Soviet Union for scientific supremacy, and beyond, to the mastery of outer space. Now, even as local, state, and federal investments in education have reached such unprecedented heights as to encounter taxpayer revolts, taxpayer expectations continue to rise. Schools are expected to shoulder even greater new responsibilities for the eradication or reduction of illiteracy, racism, drug abuse, and ecological pollution. Students from deprived backgrounds must be helped to develop positive self-concepts. Teachers and students at the secondary level (and even some elementary school pupils) demand a greater role in school governance. Pressures mount to decentralize metropolitan school systems into units subject to independent community (neighborhood) control. Experiments in accountability, "open classrooms," street academies, performance contracting, and other innovative reforms abound in widespread efforts to achieve breakthroughs in the learning process.

Teachers and others concerned with instructional needs are, consequently, deeply engaged in the search for appropriate media to use in realizing the new expectations. The search for better materials for teaching reading, for example, involves multimedia: book-and-record sets for young readers or machines which combine print and recorded voice in a new

13

approach to self-instruction. The quest may also involve reviewing and regrouping printed materials around newly defined thematic interests.

The problem of finding out what is available in certain subject fields or on topics not previously taught in the schools may appear insuperable. Imagine the perplexity involved for a young teacher who is trying to find overhead transparencies to illustrate drug abuse programs for a particular grade level, for example. The typical initial reaction of the untrained searcher is to conclude that the local user himself must produce the needed materials. But with the help of the staff of an educational media selection center, the teacher or curriculum supervisor may find the range of choices wider and more pertinent than had been anticipated. If supplementary local production is still required, at least it can be more precisely targeted.

School decentralization into districts with varying degrees of autonomy means, in many instances, that central services have been closed down or reassigned to district or regional offices. Accordingly, evaluation and procurement of instructional media cease to be carried on for all the schools in the system, and each district is faced with assuming these functions for itself, thus increasing the need for an accessible educational media selection center.

With teachers assuming greater decision-making authority for curriculum development—often as a result of union-negotiated contracts, for the evaluation and adoption of textbooks, and for the allocation of funds for related materials, the 1969 *Standards for School Media Programs* drawn up by the American Association of School Librarians and the National Education Association's Department of Audiovisual Instruction (now Association for Educational Communications and Technology) have become increasingly significant and achieving them now involves a broader constituency.

All of the foregoing developments mean a diffusion of authority for selecting educational media. What chiefly relates to the function of the educational media selection center is this: The urgency of public demand on the school has been accompanied by a decentralization that leaves the subdistrict, the individual school, and the teacher without the help that once might have been available for review and evaluation of instructional media. The lack of media training and sophistication on the part of many local budget controllers in the subdistricts and individual school may also contribute to unwise or uninformed purchases. Decentralization should mean, of course, that more users necessarily will be involved in the process of selection. Centers will provide the new kind of centralized help users need, instead of hit-or-miss reliance on partial information available in separate districts or from sales representatives of book publishers and producers of audiovisual materials.

14

The implications of "accountability" and "performance contracting" are also key factors supporting the center concept. Both fiscal methods are being adopted in communities where schools have been under pressure to respond more quickly to demands for change and improvement. More specific definitions of teaching objectives are major targets in these schemes. The application of cost accounting to instructional methods is also being tested, on the premise that better planning and budgeting will lead to more predictable results.

Under performance contracting, some aspects of teaching are assigned to commercial firms willing to "guarantee" results or forego payment for services. What the growth of performance contracting means to media selection poses fundamental policy questions, since many of the firms conducting such programs also produce their own materials, thus limiting both the choice of actual media and the responsibility for continuous, broadscale review, evaluation, and selection of the best or most appropriate media. Whether the results of performance contracting outweigh its risks and limitations in terms of the learning process will be increasingly surveyed and debated.

All of these experiments affect the selection and use of media. Some ventures, based on the conviction that more carefully prepared and/or assembled learning resources will assure improvements, include computer-assisted instruction, with or without individual dial-access terminals, multi-media packages, and systems approaches to teaching. Other experiments presume that physical or architectural environmental improvements will enhance or accelerate desired change, sometimes ignoring the intellectual and attitudinal climate of the school so vital to the learning process.

Media selection as an ongoing process is very much in the minds of educators today. A recent statement by the Association for Supervision and Curriculum Development defines four assumptions arising from the trend toward "instructional units" or "related items, usually purchased as an entity." These assumptions are:

> Increasingly, the local decision makers are faced with the task of selecting and curricularizing instructional units rather than beginning from scratch and designing them.

> The units are becoming increasingly complex and sophisticated, requiring more study and more assistance in their appraisal.

> The instructional units usually require a substantial outlay and usually will need to be used over a period of several years; therefore, careful consideration of these decisions becomes more essential than ever. Also, a growing tendency for local communities to reject

increased taxation is turning school officials toward better utilization and accountability procedures.

Local school officials need specific guidelines to assist them in reaching educational sound decisions about such units.[1]

GREATER COMMUNITY CONCERN

The value of "Sesame Street" in preparing children for school may still be debated, but there is no question about the historical importance of this television series as an example of heightened social concern for better education. For the first time, public television has been used for direct teaching on the medium's own terms. Many other agencies of society are also experimenting with a variety of developments outside the traditional educational structure, thus increasing lay experience with media for teaching purposes and the further need for assistance in media evaluation, selection, and use.

One of the most rapid developments has been the downward expansion of educational programs below the first grade. Under the impetus of federal subsidy, compensatory (Head Start) programs for disadvantaged children have been established by a variety of official agencies: public and independent schools and several agencies created to meet across-the-board needs of the poor.

Work with young children from culturally impoverished backgrounds has also attracted the interest and energies of numerous nongovernmental groups. In many communities, churches and women's organizations have set up compensatory programs for young children, staffing their centers in most cases with volunteer aides, some of them trained to teach. The untrained, however, are anxious to find out what they can about media and materials that might be used with the children in their charge. They should be provided with a place or places to examine materials and learn to use them effectively.

The downward extension of schooling has been accelerated by the changing status of women in the employment market. As more and more young married women have moved into fulltime employment, day care and nursery school enterprises have multiplied. The sponsors of these enterprises vary. Churches and women's groups have long been involved in small-scale efforts to meet the needs of working mothers. Some nurseries have been

[1] Richard I. Miller, *Selecting New Aids to Teaching* (Washington, D.C., Assn. for Supervision and Curriculum Development, 1971), p.1–2.

operated by businesses, more particularly in wartime, for their own employees. There is some evidence that public schools may eventually increase their care for preschool children.

But most of the programs for preschool-age children are offered by individuals or organizations providing a needed service for profit, though legislation providing federal support for public facilities has been introduced. Most of these business undertakings are small in scale and staffed by relatively untrained personnel, many of them greatly in need of help in evaluating, selecting, and planning for the best use of educational media. The expected growth potential of child care services has recently begun to attract business interest on a large scale: some fifty firms are currently reportedly engaged in franchising or "packaging" day care centers. As in the case of performance contractors, some provide their own materials. Persons working with young children in this relatively new field need a community media service not now generally available to them.

An increase in adult education facilities and service is another indication of greater community concern for the quality and range of education, reflected by new support for such long-established and publicly sponsored programs as those in career education and by a variety of less familiar opportunities.

The construction of new, federally funded, multicounty or regional schools across the nation has given new impetus to vocational education in the past decade. Rapid changeovers in job requirements mean that many workers must return to school during their employment careers to retrain for new assignments. Enlarged schools will extend their services to post-secondary students of all ages. Labor unions are including demands for funds for the continuing education of their members in contract negotiations.

The principle that education should be made available to learners of all ages is well recognized in existing adult continuing-education programs provided by public schools and other agencies. In the past, support of these programs has often been justified by the provision of courses enabling persons with interrupted high school education to complete their credits for graduation. More recently the trend has been toward centers where adults may come in for instruction, often individualized, to fill a much broader range of educational needs and interests.

Special programs for adults include opportunities for the aged, sometimes in connection with recreational programs, but also as a service available to senior citizens in the many new, privately or publicly operated residential complexes for persons in retirement. The courses generally include classes in arts and crafts as well as leisure-time activities. Courses that serve the health and sometimes the financial needs of the aged are also frequently provided, as are courses in current events and world affairs.

The growth of volunteer tutoring as a part of the effort to improve the lot of children living in the inner city has also led to new demands for adult education. Professionals, paraprofessionals, and volunteers all need to know where to find appropriate materials for both the tutors and the mothers of the children involved.

In short, the upward extension of continuing education into the adult and senior-citizen years, and the downward expansion into the preschool group, greatly enlarges the number of persons, both instructors and consumers, that the educational media selection centers would serve, directly or indirectly.

The decentralization of authority in urban school systems is the most dramatic and widely publicized example of a new pattern of lay participation in educational policy making and operations. The objective is to achieve, in the decision-making process, a more accurate reflection of the immediate community's various needs. Each of the eight districts in Detroit, for example, has its own school board, empowered to make most key decisions, with the central board of education serving chiefly as overseer and umpire. Each district is encouraged to develop policies and programs which serve the particular needs of its own students.

Lay involvement in curriculum planning in these newly decentralized school systems usually occurs in ways unique to local needs and circumstances, but a few general trends are evident.

One of these is the development of programs relating to racial or ethnic identity. Early in the deliberate efforts to build a sense of pride in young members of minority groups, programs were created and conducted outside established school systems. After-school and Saturday morning classes were modeled more or less on similarly conducted religious-education programs. The sponsorship and staffing, more often than not, were entirely in lay hands. As could have been predicted, the search for educational media to use in these ventures was often as desperate as it was uninformed.

Now, schools serving members of racial or ethnic minorities are increasingly expected to provide a curriculum responsive to the need to understand differing cultural heritages. This emphasis in the regular school curriculum has also encouraged the production of many kinds of new and useful study materials. The role of the lay person, nonetheless, remains crucial in helping school personnel define and apply content criteria in the review process, and also to identify gaps and new possibilities in program planning.

Another form of lay involvement is the rapid growth of small experimental schools outside the educational establishment. Organized by teachers who may have felt themselves hampered by tradition-bound schools and by parents who prefer a new kind of schooling for their children, such "free" schools are springing up in many communities.

18

Lay involvement in school operations, although long a basic principle of public education in this country, has never before been such an influential factor in planning and affecting what happens in the schools. Consequently, the need to provide the kinds of services envisioned by the fully equipped educational media selection center becomes even more obviously important to community well-being in its broadest social sense.

3

Center Administration

Two major elements determine the administration of educational media selection centers: (1) The governance of the center, i.e., the legal basis of the framework for its administration and the structure of its relationships with participating agencies, public or private; and (2) the management of the center, i.e., systematic ways and means of program development and operation to achieve the center's objectives.

GOVERNANCE OF THE CENTER

The governance of a center will be determined by the nature of the supportive agencies to be served and by the applicable local, state, and federal legislative provisions. An educational media selection center is comparable to other library or similar educational service agencies in this respect. Governance that involves or anticipates a local, regional, or state-level network of centers (p. 73 ff.) would pose an additional statutory and administrative challenge, which should be confronted squarely at the planning stage.

The need for new and imaginative governance patterns to provide more effectively for educational services has been recognized. The variation in state governments within the United States complicates the design of an administrative structure affecting cooperation among the states.

Charles L. Willis (program officer for the Development of Educational Activities, Dayton, Ohio) has written about emerging administrative patterns and procedures affecting educational services:

> America's search for structural designs and administrative arrangements which will provide more adequate educational services reflects the character of decentralized government. Most accurate

observations about this search will include the concept of variability.[1]

These variations include very simple or very complicated provisions for the governance of an educational media selection center, depending on the nature of the operation. Its governance may be generally defined within the scope of existing law and administrative regulations when it is intended to serve chiefly the needs of one school system, or when one agency contracts with others to provide services. Indeed, the center may be interpreted in some situations as a logical extension of the educational program already operating under general statutory provisions for such programs and not requiring specific authorization in law. On the other hand, it may require complex legal definition involving new legislative authorization if it is to serve a number of school or library systems, private agencies, or varying combinations of these, or if it is to cut across the traditional lines of district, county, or state boundaries, or be a network component.

Mr. Willis has reported on the trend in school administration toward establishing intermediate administrative units:

> Another effort to combat inadequacies of school districts with limited enrollments has resulted in the establishment of an administrative level between the state and a number of local districts. This level is generally termed an intermediate school administrative unit; its organizational arrangements have taken various forms to fulfill supervisory and/or special service functions. In addition to administration of traditional elementary and secondary school programs, the intermediate unit or similar regional organizations are used for operating selected elements of the educational program, such as technical-vocational schools and community junior colleges.[2]

This trend has obvious implications for the establishment of centers at this intermediate administrative level.

In discussing the legal provisions for libraries in the United States, Roy M. Mersky has said:

> The legal basis for the existence of libraries in the United States thus may be found in state constitutions, or in laws enacted by state legislatures, in court decisions, opinions of attorneys general, and administrative rulings of specific state agencies. The body of law establishes the basic contemporary framework for the administration

[1] "Emerging Patterns of School District Organization with Implications for School Library Service," *Library Trends* 16:429 (April 1968).

[2] Ibid., p.429–30.

of programs of library services. It determines the general conditions under which publicly supported libraries may operate and authorizes the expenditure of tax funds for library services. Some of the libraries so established are essential components of public schools and colleges; others are indispensable supplements to governmental agencies; still others are independent institutions for the dissemination of knowledge to the general public.[3]

These opinions relate to the governance of a center which may be defined for legal purposes as a specialized type of library or information media program. Since no two of the fifty states have identical legal provisions for education or for libraries, centers serving more than one state will be challenged to consider provisions in existing interstate educational compacts or to initiate enactment of legislation to achieve new purposes.

A consideration of the variety of agencies, institutions, organizations, or individuals that would find the services of an educational media selection center potentially valuable illustrates the difficulty of suggesting any single pattern for an administrative structure that will provide them access to the center and its services and fairly allocate responsibility for financial support and for administration. Some possible components of such a system include:

1. A local public school system (district, city, county, parish)
2. A local public library system (municipal, county, regional)
3. A state-supported college or university which educates teachers, librarians, or other media specialists
4. An intermediate school administrative unit at a level between the state and several school systems
5. A state education department
6. A state library agency
7. A state system of higher education
8. A nonpublic elementary and/or secondary school
9. A nonpublic college or university which educates teachers, librarians and/or media specialists
10. A system of nonpublic schools
11. A system of nonpublic colleges or universities
12. Profit-making corporations related to the knowledge industry: publishers and producers of instructional media
13. Governmental or nonprofit private agencies at all levels concerned with institutional care of children or young people
14. Professional societies and associations concerned with instructional design, media production and use
15. A network of centers at the local, regional, and state levels.

[3] "Library Laws," *Encyclopedia Americana.*

22

Since the purposes and functions of a center might be achieved by one or many combinations of these auspices, no one pattern of governance can be recommended as a general guide for all situations. The governance for *any* center, however, must be clearly established by statute, charter, or contract.

Major legal provisions include: (1) authorization for establishment of the center, specifying the governmental or other organizations so empowered; (2) establishment or identification of a body to exercise administrative control over the center; and (3) appropriation of continuing funds. When a center represents a cooperative effort involving public and/or private agencies or a combination of political units, the legislative provisions must spell out the nature of such cooperation, showing the allocation of authority and responsibilities.

A variety of feasible arrangements for cooperative governance of a center exists. Among them are: (1) federation of participating agencies, not completely integrated governmentally but with a representative governing board; (2) cooperative arrangement in which the participating agencies agree to conditions of governance and provide varying degrees of financial support; and (3) contractual agreement stipulating conditions, controls, and payment for services, in which one agency assumes the major responsibilities and provides services for one or more participating units.

The identification of the best administrative pattern for a center will be dependent upon the imagination and resourcefulness of the planners, with full consideration of statutory limitations or potentials. The planning team or task force, especially if a consortium is involved, should be broadly representative of the sponsoring agencies and user groups.

MANAGEMENT OF THE CENTER

The Wheeler and Goldhor definition of the term *administration* in public libraries is relevant here:

> It means essentially the directing that gets the job done. It involves comprehending purposes, needs and opportunities. Planning, defining problems, making decisions, finding ways and means, managing and following through. Organizing; or recognizing and defining, then putting together in sound and simple relationship the component elements or decisions of the operation as a whole, then of its smaller parts—departments and individual jobs. Selection of personnel; the understanding, choosing and appreciation of people and their development. Assigning work according to abilities, with judgment and consideration in fitting them together. Defining re-

23

sponsibilities and lines of authority. Giving instructions. Supervising the guidance of those for whose work one is responsible, seeing that each does his work with distinction . . . scrutinizing and evaluating, and measuring results, in terms of reader (user) satisfaction, with attention to costs.[4]

If this description of administration is accepted, the director of an educational media selection center has, clearly, a catalytic as well as leadership role in terms of the administrative and management responsibilities and functions involved in (1) coordination of sponsorship, (2) negotiation of funding, (3) design and construction of physical facilities, and (4) program planning, staffing, and evaluation.

A governing board is formed, representing the unit and agency or agencies principally responsible for the governance of the center. Where there is multiple sponsorship, the planning team or task force should be consulted in the selection of a center director. Otherwise, the appointment is made by the individual agency involved after consultation with other agencies expected to use the center.

An advisory board, representing the variety of interests and concerns of the center's clientele, should participate in recommending long-range objectives and in evaluating achievement of these objectives. Where there is multiple sponsorship this board can be formed from the initial planning group.

The administrative responsibilities and their assignment to the director and the two boards are shown in table 1.

For the director of a center, working with his staff and advisory board, planning will be a most important responsibility. It assumes even greater significance if the center serves a variety of users representing several agencies or institutions, all of whom should be consulted to identify the needs of users of the center. As the program develops, there should be continuous evaluation to determine the extent of achievement of objectives, reasons for lack of achievement, and ways and means of improvement. It should also take into consideration new methods or restatement of objectives. To the extent that it is feasible, all those affected by a center's services should have opportunities to suggest improvements.

As the concepts of accountability and assessment are increasingly implemented in education, centers will be required to define their programs in terms of performance objectives that are measurable. Leadership in achieving this definition, within terms yet to be developed, will be a responsibility of the center's director.

[4] Joseph L. Wheeler and Herbert Goldhor, *Practical Administration of Public Libraries* (New York: Harper & Row, 1962), p.35.

Table 1. ALLOCATION OF ADMINISTRATIVE
RESPONSIBILITIES

GOVERNING BOARD

1. Making policy
2. Approving long- and short-range plans
3. Authorizing personnel appointments or transfer from other cooperating agencies
4. Procuring and allocating funds to support a program to achieve objectives
5. Interpreting the center's program, achievements, and needs to public and private agencies where pertinent to gain support.

ADVISORY BOARD

1. Recommending policy or policy changes or responding to such recommendations from governing board or director
2. Recommending program objectives or services
3. Serving as liaison between the center and its clientele, interpreting the center, and reflecting users' needs, interests, and concerns
4. Serving as "sounding board" for the director and staff.

DIRECTOR OF CENTER

1. Leading the staff, the advisory and governing boards in defining objectives, determining policies and programs, and measuring achievement
2. Recommending staff appointments
3. Developing the professional and paraprofessional staff through supervision and inservice education
4. Managing finance, including budgeting, accounting procedures and records
5. Organizing internal operations in the center, including work definition and assignment and supervisory responsibilities (in cooperation with appropriate staff)
6. Building the center's collections and related services to meet users' needs
7. Controlling and maintaining educational media according to adopted policy about use
8. Supervising facilities to effect their best use and to identify needed improvements
9. Designing an inservice education program for the center's clientele
10. Identifying and interpreting the center's achievements, problems, and needs as a means to its improvement
11. Maintaining proper relationships with those who use and those who govern the center, to encourage understanding of the center's program, potential, and needs.

4

The Center Program

The educational media selection center should provide a planned program of direct and indirect assistance to users in identifying, obtaining, examining, and evaluating educational media for a variety of learning purposes.

Although particular emphasis and applications of function will be influenced by such factors as the governance of a given center, its clientele, and the role of the center vis-à-vis services offered by the agencies from which users come, certain areas of program functions are common responsibilities of all centers. These areas include: (1) reference/information and consultant service to users, (2) evaluation of media, (3) provision of inservice training for users, (4) research, and (5) communications (public relations and information-sharing programs).

REFERENCE AND CONSULTANT SERVICE

The reference and consultant service, both direct and indirect, should be flexible and responsive to user needs. A few examples illustrate this point.

When a group of sixth-grade teachers call the center accessible to their school system to make a date to see new materials in black studies appropriate for their grade level, in order to determine what materials could supplement a textbook, they should be able to schedule the use of the media they will need for this purpose, including preview rooms, and secure a consultant to meet with them. They should be able to do this with one telephone call, note, or visit, rather than a series of requests directed to various staff members.

When a university instructor in the teaching of reading wishes to schedule a class session at the center serving his campus to permit students to survey elementary-level materials and gain experience in identifying approximate reading levels, his request should be considered appropriate. The center staff should encourage him also to consider additional uses of the center.

When a new superintendent of a school system which participates in a cooperative EMSC requests clarification of the function and purpose of the center, he should personally be given information about the variety of media displayed in the center, the extent of the staff's involvement in inservice programs (with special reference to those appropriate for the staff in his system), and the range of informational materials available about the center itself.

Similarly, the center staff should be ready to assist the program director of a neighborhood youth group to select materials that support or enrich the group's remedial or recreational activities.

The kind, level, and amount of assistance provided to users varies with user purposes and needs. Provision should be made by the center to perform the following services for users (whether individuals or groups):

1. Plan for hospitable "floor service" so that visitors to the center are welcomed and assisted, as needed, in its use. Staff members should be alert to spot a perplexed user, make the person feel free to ask for assistance, and offer help to those who need help but are reticent to ask for it.

2. Provide information services to individual users in response to telephone, mail, and face-to-face requests: in particular, answer queries about sources of media, addresses of vendors, and the like. In addition, the EMSC may well serve as a switching center of information concerning evaluation and selection activities of user groups, maintaining for this purpose directory information on administrators, consultants, media specialists, and evaluators within the user agencies.

3. Schedule use of media (materials and equipment), appropriate space in which to examine them, and assistance from a staff member in their use. Provision should be made for media and staff help to be available on occasion outside the center itself, as in conjunction with workshop sessions.

4. Prepare and plan for group work in evaluation of media for a specified purpose by retrieving media from the collection for examination, obtaining additional media needed for review, checking sources and reference tools that may offer further assistance, and compiling preliminary checklists of media for use by the group.

5. Work with a group of users in their examination of media in the center by demonstrating the use or operation of particular materials or equipment, presenting a discussion of evaluation criteria for the purpose at hand, and participating in preview sessions to appraise materials.

6. Offer consultant help as needs are identified. For example, a media specialist in the EMSC may note in a school system curriculum bulletin that a committee is considering the introduction of a new approach to in-

struction in foreign languages; get in touch with the committee chairman to ask for information to offer to assist the committee in its work, and (even if no continuing relationship is established) to call to the committee's attention the criteria being used in EMSC's evaluation of foreign language media. The center specialist invites feedback and asks to be informed of any recommendations the committee might make to change or improve the center.

7. Anticipate the needs of users by identifying educational changes and trends in curriculum development; and monitor the introduction of new media.

8. Encourage participation by EMSC staff members on committees appointed by agencies that support and use the center, and in meetings and programs sponsored by agencies, as observers or as speakers, combined with frequent visits to schools, libraries, or other institutions represented by center users, in order to keep informed of needs for and uses of media.

Indirect assistance to center users, another important continuing function, is provided by center-prepared publications and the dissemination of information materials. Examples include: preparation and distribution on a regular basis of lists of new media received, as well as special lists compiled to serve particular needs; announcements of special media exhibits; bulletins about the center's services; and guides showing locations of the collections in the center.

This communications function transcends normal public information procedures. The selective dissemination of information should be a principal objective of the center's program. Special interest profiles of major users should be constructed and kept up-to-date so that, by whatever method is appropriate and feasible (manual or machine aided), individuals can be notified whenever the center acquires relevant new media or evaluations of new media in special-interest fields. This function has a dual purpose, since these people can and should be called upon to help evaluate specialized materials about which they have expertise.

EVALUATION

Evaluation is, simply, a means for ascertaining the value of something. Applied to media, the task involves appraisal of an item of instructional material in terms of its assets, limitations, and intended use. Effective evaluation, of course, implies that appraisal is done by persons who are sensitive to the needs of users and who can interpret and report reactions from the field. The proliferation of the number and kinds of instructional designs, reflecting both the enormous mass of information generated by technology and the new technology of information transfer, has created demands for more precise and effective evaluation of media in relation to its appropriateness for specified instructional purposes. As noted earlier, trends in contemporary instruction stress independent study, small-group interaction, large-group instruction, simulation, and other learning configurations. The evaluation of media must convey information concerning the usefulness of materials for these diverse instructional methods. If it is to be of maximum effectiveness to the user, an evaluation program should comprehend educational trends, new techniques, and media innovations. In this respect the evaluation program of the educational media selection center is inextricably related to its inservice education function.

A basic function of each center is systematic evaluation and selection of media for its own use. A principal product of this task is the collection and preparation of descriptive information about media and their relationship to varieties of teaching/learning developments.

An effective center would be a link in a larger evaluation system and a switching center in the projected network of centers outlined in chapter 9. As such, a local center's function is not to evaluate the total universe of educational media and resources, especially the major instructional systems designed for basal adoption and use throughout an entire school system. Before defining more precisely what is the specific evaluation component of a center's program, the dimensions and characteristics of evaluation as a concept and process should be clarified.

Dimensions of Evaluation. Evaluation of educational media analyzes materials in terms of two broad and interrelated elements: the intrinsic qualities of materials and factors affecting their use. An evaluation process incorporates three stages or levels of analysis: preliminary appraisal of materials, pilot testing of materials, and evaluation of effectiveness in actual use.

Preliminary appraisal of materials yields these basic descriptive data:

1. Identifying (bibliographic) information, e.g., author, title, publisher/producer, date, place of publication.

2. Format information, e.g., the medium and physical description of the item (number of frames, reels, speed, color, size or, for books, whether hardcover, paperbound, looseleaf, graphics, etc.).

3. Design information, e.g., the mode of presentation (programmed instruction, tape, film) and whether the unit is self-contained or part of a system.

Preliminary appraisal permits analysis of materials in terms of criteria specifying acceptable levels of quality in content, in design, and in presentation. It includes prediction of potential use of the material by the intended audience as identified by the publisher or producer, the appraiser's knowledge of the needs of the target group and of effective instructional applications, and the relationship of the media being evaluated to that already tested and in use.

In many instances available information may be insufficient to enable the user to fit a particular item into an instructional presentation. Given such a limitation, field testing of materials is needed to determine potentially effective uses of media. An effective field-testing system will satisfy the following criteria:

Is the age group used for field testing appropriate to the material?
Is the sample population large enough to provide significant findings?
Are all individuals in the sample population at the same entry level?
Are there control groups to compare with test groups?

The results of preliminary appraisal and field testing remain predictive until validated by evaluation of the use of materials in an actual instructional presentation—the final level of the evaluation process. Common sense indicates, however, that, if there were total dependence on this final level, the process would be eternal. Materials would be suspended in the predictive stage of evaluation until they were superseded or became obsolete. In short, preliminary tests may have to be accepted, especially with respect to materials in relatively traditional formats. Field testing and evaluation may blend and be combined.

Role of the EMSC in Evaluation. The functions of the educational media selection center and its staff in the evaluation process include: the collection and organization of materials for examination; the capture and dissemination of published evaluations of media; the development and provision of improved criteria and data forms to gather responses from users, who are encouraged to record their use of materials after applying them in real situations; arranging for user evaluations (assignment of persons and media, assistance and guidance), collecting and organizing the resulting data; and dissemination of the findings on a timely basis.

Users of the center need, ideally, total access to professional literature on the selection and evaluation of educational media: selection policies used by school and public library systems; books, articles, and reports that offer guidelines for evaluation of materials in particular subjects or educational programs (such as multimedia materials on various ethnic groups); media for partially sighted and other handicapped children, and for other vocational and career education; and comprehensive treatments of the selection and evaluation of materials and equipment in each of the various formats.

Such resources form part of the supporting collection of the EMSC, as does an extensive collection of publications offering information about sources of supply, reviews, and evaluations of educational media; selected publishers', wholesalers', and producers' catalogs; trade bibliographic and announcement services; general and specialized lists and bibliographies of recommended materials; and reviewing sources. Total access is not likely to be achieved in every center's initial, organizational stage. Indeed, it may not be achieved at all in the absence of the cooperative network recommended later in this report. But selected dissemination of information procedures should and can be organized at once.

To promote validity and consistency in evaluation, the center should publish and distribute statements of criteria, as well as response forms on which evaluations are recorded. The content, scope, sequence, format, etc., of the evaluation response form should take into account such questions as:

What data can be supplied routinely by the center staff, as a function of the acquisitions process (e.g., basic entry data for the material, derived from trade sources and validated by inspection of the item on receipt)?

How can responses requested from evaluators be simply recorded (for the benefit of the respondent and those who will need to tabulate and analyze the data, i.e., consider forms that permit a checkmark rather than a narrative response)?

What depth of information can be justified in terms of utility? feasibility?

What elements of the evaluation, as recorded on the response form, are capable of machine manipulation to provide printouts as by-products?

How can compatibility be achieved in the response forms used in different educational media selection centers, and what degree of consistency is needed to enable centers to share evaluations and participate in networking approaches to the evaluation program?

Dissemination of the results of evaluation of educational media completes the process. Facilities must include:

A storage and retrieval system that affords consistent, convenient access to evaluations (response forms)—preferably with multiple points of entry

Means for updating and making known a variety of evaluative viewpoints based upon subsequent use data

Capability to produce listings (manually or machine aided) based on evaluations, as needed to serve various purposes of users (e.g., bibliographies that group materials by subject/level/mode of use dimensions)

Capability to share evaluations (economically and when needed) as part of a network of educational media selection centers.

Developing an Evaluation Program. An effective evaluation program should be responsive to the following questions:

Do guidelines established for evaluation specify clearly the nature of the information required by the center?

Does the evaluation of materials give highest priority to the fact that the media must satisfy learning needs?

Do the evaluators represent a cross section of relevant professional competencies?

On the nature of evaluation, Erikson says:

> The inexperienced and incompetent have no business doing the important work of evaluation. Evaluation is a critical function and one that carries with it a heavy responsibility. The decisions to accept or reject and to rate high or rate low are in a real sense a public display of competence or incompetence. It must be remembered that producers of materials deserve to be treated fairly, and that to choose poor quality materials is not only a waste of public money but also a source of potential educational injury to learners. . . .
>
> . . . two levels of selection should be identified. The first is at the classroom teaching level. At this level the teacher selects from local or remote sources for a forthcoming unit and carries out an appropriate pre-use examination. The second level of selection is the system-wide, central distribution level. At this level the director of instructional media services must assume responsibility for selection of the best materials that teachers need to carry on their work effectively. The best basis for selection of materials at both levels is their probable contribution to valid teaching purposes (these of course being the best possible estimates of pupil needs), their excellence in technical quality, and their suitability for known groups of learners. The only valid reason for selection at the second level is to facilitate selection at the first. The director himself must therefore be able to evaluate materials for selection and to teach others this skill, and he must be successful in obtaining the willing services of teachers in setting up sound policy and in getting the work of evaluation and selection done as efficiently as possible. The sub-

jective nature of the task of evaluation demands a usable set of criteria—usable, that is, in terms of effectiveness and convenience.[1]

Further questions include:

Does the center gather and apply information about new trends, innovations, and approaches to learning in the evaluation of materials?

Does the evaluation system provide for feedback from users based on their experience with materials?

Is the feedback from user experience applied constructively to improve the evaluation process?

Is the evaluation information precise enough to be handled and transferred with relative ease and timeliness?

Does the report form and frequency provide adequate information to users when they need it?

Does the evaluation information provided meet the needs of the users effectively? efficiently? Is it sufficiently succinct and relevant to assist users in applying materials to instructional approaches?

Does the method of communicating evaluation information keep to a minimum the time lag between the generation of information and its dissemination?

Are incoming items compared with those evaluated earlier, even if the media are no longer in the center?

The center's evaluation functions should be clearly defined. In summary, the center assists users, individually or in groups, to identify, appraise, and select media for potential use in relation to specific courses or informal educational programs. The center systematically collects, organizes, and disseminates professional evaluations of new education media; it evaluates such media for its *own* use or for demonstration purposes; and it may, whenever appropriate and depending on its governance, *initiate* evaluations of media in specific subject areas or forms of media, preferably as part of a network.

The limitations of the evaluation function should also be clearly understood by staff and users. An evaluation, as considered here, is an informed, professional, critical report on what a particular item offers to potential users; evaluations compiled and disseminated by a center do not constitute a buying guide (even though they are often used as such). They do, however, make it possible for informed professional judgments to be made about media for potential purchase. Centers do not operate to recommend

---

[1] Carlton W. H. Erickson, *Administering Instructional Media Programs* (New York: Macmillan, 1968), p.65–66.

33

one or two items in a category of media, but rather to satisfy users' needs for access to evaluations and to provide a place where media can be examined and where people can be trained in their use.

Approaches to the organization of the evaluation function—recruitment and "assignment" of evaluators, assignment of media for evaluation—are shaped by the administrative structure of the particular center, its clientele, and practices within the agencies represented by this clientele. In fulfilling its evaluation function, a center may find that a nucleus exists in school system curriculum committees, in review committees of school media specialists and of public library children's and young adult librarians: many appropriate patterns may be found. Other resources in teacher education institutions or specialized research institutes may be tapped to mutual advantage. Whatever specific approaches are used, the assignment of responsibility for evaluation should assure continuous, systematic appraisal of new media; division of responsibility (probably by subject, grade, and learning level combinations) to enable evaluators to work in or develop areas of special competence; inclusion of persons with current experience in using media with children and young adults in educational and community settings; and a broad base of representation among the center's user groups. Voluntary participation in evaluation should be sought and encouraged, as should the use of expert consultants in areas of special needs.

Procedures used to select evaluators, the assignment of media to them, and continuing critical review of their evaluations should be clearly defined and interpreted. The same is true of policies for encouraging and handling "volunteered" evaluations. Policies must be made and interpreted about the distribution of new media to evaluators for examination and field testing outside the center.

INSTRUCTION

Continuing-education experiences both for staff members and for users of educational media selection centers are essential elements in developing a program of service in these centers. Elizabeth Stone suggests that continuing professional education "includes everything that is learned between pre-service education and professional retirement," and notes that "although continuing education involves a much longer span than pre-service education, until recently its great importance has scarcely been recognized by the library profession."[2]

[2] "Continuing Education: Avenue to Adventure," *School Libraries* 18:38 (Summer, 1969).

One of the primary functions of the educational media selection center is to provide instruction to its users to help them become increasingly proficient in the evaluation, selection, and use of media.

Among the elements that must be present in any successful program of inservice education, planning is of the first importance. Meierhenry states that inservice experiences "must be deliberately planned with purposes and functions to be met rather than developed haphazardly, incidentally, or not at all."[3] Harris has said, "if it weren't violated so much in practice, it would seem too obvious to require mentioning that the first task of designing a program is to get clearly in mind what the program is to achieve. When this has been done it seems equally elementary to suggest that the next step is to discover some means for reaching the desired outcome."[4]

Virginia McJenkin has proposed the following guidelines for planning inservice-education programs, guidelines that, while geared to programs for teachers and other public school personnel, are equally applicable to programs planned for any group of users served by the educational media selection center:

The program must grow out of problems that are significant to teachers, librarians, supervisors, and principals.

The concerned persons must be involved in planning the inservice activities.

There must be opportunities for all concerned to share effective techniques that are learned and materials that are located.

Necessary resources, materials, and consultants must be made available.

Any program must start where the group is and go as far as possible.

Each person must have a vital part in making the program successful.

There must be evaluation of the program and re-examination of needs at regular intervals.[5]

The first guideline specifies that the inservice program must grow out of needs that are significant to the users. These needs may be identified by

[3] W. C. Meierhenry, *Media Competencies for Teachers:* A Project to Identify Competencies Needed by Teachers in the Use of the Newer Media and Various Approaches to Achieving Them (Lincoln: University of Nebraska, 1966), p.219 (ED-012-713).

[4] Ben Harris, *In-Service Education: A Guide to Better Practice* (Englewood Cliffs, N.J.: Prentice-Hall, 1969), p.30.

[5] "School System Programs of In-Service Education on the School Library as a Materials Center," in *The School Library as a Materials Center*, ed. by Mary Helen Mahar, Office of Education, Publication no. OE-15042 (Washington: Govt. Printing Office, 1963) p.35–40.

the center staff, by the users themselves, or by consultants called in to evaluate the work of the center. For example, if evaluations made of new media by users of an EMSC indicate that the evaluators are unaware of the range of materials available which are similar in scope or purpose, the center staff may initiate a workshop for evaluators to point out what is currently available and to review prevailing criteria in the light of new knowledge. In this way, users will gain judgmental experience and become potentially effective evaluators.

A second element that gives vitality to inservice education is that all persons concerned with the training program must share in its planning. Too often a selected few determine needs and plan a program to satisfy them, forgetting that "those who share, care," and they fail to involve the ultimate participants or consumers in the decision-making process. The persons concerned include both potential participants and other persons in the particular administrative structure who share responsibilities for the media program. In the case of a school system-based educational media selection center, for example, the persons concerned would include the district media director, media specialists, and administrative personnel with direct responsibilities for the performance of the participants.

Identification of objectives to be accomplished is a third essential element in planning inservice programs. Specific objectives give focus to the program. Objectives for a given program must reflect the expectations of participants and be geared to their level of understanding.

The content of specific inservice education programs obviously grows out of local definition of needs and objectives. As a general rule, emphasis should be given to firsthand experience—opportunities for participants to handle and use materials and equipment and to experiment with techniques. A first imperative is to allow ample lead time for planning, well in advance of the beginning of the program.

Adequate support, in the form of staff, consultant help, and media resources for the inservice effort, is obviously important. It would be unrealistic to expect the staff of a center to have all competencies necessary to direct and staff all inservice programs conducted. Arrangements should be made for obtaining appropriate consultant help from media specialists and others in school and public library systems, colleges and universities, and other agencies within and outside the community served. Such external involvement also promotes their use of the center. Resources (materials and equipment) to support a given inservice program must be determined, and any gaps filled by purchase, loan, and/or local production of materials if absolutely necessary.

The format and techniques of the program grow from objectives and content. For example, operation of a new piece of equipment may be demonstrated and practiced in a single session; inservice education in

36

selection of materials for a given subject area or target group may require meetings at frequent intervals over an extended time to allow for examination, appraisal, arrangements for field testing, sharing results, and reaching decisions.

The staff needed to conduct inservice programs must be determined on the basis of competencies, the program content and objectives, and the number of participants. Responsibilities must be defined, and specific assignments made.

The choice of location for the inservice program should be based on convenience to participants, considering such factors as travel time, traffic patterns, parking, and the availability of quarters and supporting resources (funds and materials) appropriate to the activities planned. Other factors being equal, use of the center itself is preferred.

Probably the most critical element in conducting inservice programs is the evaluation of program results. How fully have the program objectives and the expectations of participants been met? Initial planning of the inservice program must include provisions for evaluation, especially while the program is being conducted, in order to determine whether participants are moving toward their goals and whether changes in content, sequence, scheduling, or emphasis may be needed. Evidence of changes in participants' preferences for certain media, at the expense of others, and their application of skills learned are tests of program effectiveness. The evaluation design seeks ways to determine such results through follow-up studies.

Of the more than twenty inservice approaches and methods identified by respondents to an inquiry in the EMSC Program Phase I report, the six most frequently mentioned were: workshops, programs conducted at meetings, orientation programs, displays and exhibits, demonstrations, and conferences. Other approaches included extension courses, sessions for preview of materials, field trips, materials production activities, media review groups, and seminars. The following examples of experiences in continuing education illustrate strategies used in educational media selection centers:

1. Self-instruction laboratories are used to provide ongoing opportunities for individualized instruction in the operation of media equipment. Permanent stations are outfitted with essential equipment and a manual of step-by-step instructions for equipment use. The self-instruction programs are revised as needed to make each step clearer to the learner and to reflect changes in equipment.

2. Educational television is being used to disseminate information about media in a workshop offered for credit to school personnel by a state department of education. It is also used for previewing new films available from local school system centers.

3. One state department of education is using a mobile unit to extend the services of its educational media selection center. This unit carries collections of materials to areas beyond convenient access to the center, for use in workshops on selection and use of media conducted by professional staff members from the center. Collections in the mobile unit are changed to meet specific interests, e.g., foreign languages, African studies, and state geography, history, and government. Following the workshop presentations, the mobile unit remains in the local school system for one or two weeks, where its use by local school personnel is guided by a school system coordinator.

4. A large suburban school system reports that the inservice activities most sought by teachers, principals, and librarians are workshops in the production of materials, equipment use, and effective utilization of media, including television. These workshops, conducted concurrently during the school year in fifteen sessions each, offer a combination of demonstration and firsthand experiences. Participants (twenty-five per workshop) receive salary increment credit and/or credit towards the renewal of their state certificate.

Other centers report working with a school district adult-education division or the faculty of an area college or university to provide formal continuing-education opportunities for teachers and building-level media specialists.

From information received from center directors and visiting team members in Phase I, it appears that most inservice education programs conducted by educational media selection centers have been directed to teachers and other school-related groups. Little evidence was found of efforts to determine and serve the continuing-education interests of other community groups utilizing media with children or youth. The education function should be broadened to include all relevant groups in its community.

As respondents analyzed their inservice education programs, the weaknesses identified most frequently included lack of planning or poor planning and failure to tailor programs to the expressed needs of participants. The lack of skilled staff to help plan and conduct inservice programs was another recurring problem.

Factors that contribute to the success of inservice programs, according to the Phase I report, begin with released time for participation—a recommendation that is specifically directed to school-related groups but would apply as well to employees of other organizations and agencies. Providing incentive and/or stimulus for participation in inservice experiences (such as certification credit, credit for meeting school district standards or requirements for advancement within the system, or incentive pay) were also cited. Financial support to employ personnel or consultants for inservice education was emphasized. Lack of support for inservice education may be attributable to a center's failure to identify results of such educational programs. The importance of accessibility of the center (or other location selected for use in inservice education programs) was noted, as was the need for suitable quarters.

The examples given above reflect existing experience. Those who are responsible for providing inservice education opportunities for users of educational media selection centers must look to local needs but consider them in relationship to broader-based opportunities. More traditional approaches must be balanced by creativity in response to current user interests. Aspects deserving further exploration include:

1. Possible and appropriate assistance to center users in the production and evaluation of materials needed in specific learning situations which are not otherwise available, including simpler forms of programmed instruction materials supporting individualized learning by center users

2. Use of educational community antenna television (CATV) systems in inservice education, especially where provisions for audience participation are built into the system

3. Development of effective ways, such as the mobile unit, to carry materials used in inservice programs to the place of use

4. Exploration and use of means for sharing of resources, expertise, and experience among educational media selection centers.

RESEARCH

The development of effective programs in centers will depend, in the long run, on knowing more about media, the evaluation and selection of media, and the various uses of media, as well as selection centers themselves.

The Phase I report of the EMSC Program not only reported the first extensive research related to media selection centers, but also identified areas of needed research: (1) research which applies to a broad range of centers, their governance, their relationships to one another and to their constituencies; (2) research related to their internal operation and services; and (3) research related to media which might influence the programs of selection centers.

Not every new or expanded center can be expected to plan and budget for comprehensive research as a component of its program. A research capability should be built into the program, however, so that a center can both survey aspects of its own sphere of service and contribute to broader studies undertaken and coordinated at the regional, state, and national levels, or by a network, on a continuing basis.

Research that can realistically be carried forward by an individual center includes:

1. *Services.* Planning effective center programs depends on better information concerning good internal operations and services, and on knowing the characteristics and needs of potential users of the center. Center directors need data on collections, procedures, and organization as well.

In planning center services, the director needs to know who his actual and potential users are. A useful study would identify all the possible users of the center and learn from them what services they need. It would determine what materials they want and what would motivate them to come to the center. In a center already in operation, a use study would complement the study of the potential users and serve to evaluate the program.

2. *Instruction.* In addition to identifying needed services and evaluating existing ones, a study of inservice education would also serve to establish areas. Research studies could also indicate what kinds of inservice education are most effective. It should be possible to determine whether workshops conducted at the center, videotaped demonstrations, or other techniques are most successful.

The Phase I report indicated that a pronounced bias on the part of center staff for print or for audiovisual media can affect its program. A detailed personnel study should explore the attitudes of center personnel towards different media, and should seek to determine how educational background and experience affect attitudes. The data gathered would be helpful in determining the kinds of preservice education most needed for center staff.

3. *Collections.* Research needs to be done to determine the best organizational patterns for the collection. The center director needs to know how users want the collection cataloged or arranged, whether divided in broad subject and age-level groupings or more precisely classified. Do they want the media interfiled by subject, or are they able to work more efficiently when the collection is divided by format? Such information enables the director to establish policies and procedures that make the center most valuable to its users.

A second category of further research can best be planned, funded, and coordinated at a higher organizational level, for example:

1. *Research about media.* The range of possible research about different media, their value and use, is too broad to explore in detail here. Studies

which report investigations of pupil or teacher use of media should generally be useful in planning center services. Research can include studies of how materials are used as part of the program of the schools or other agencies which the centers serve, but EMSCs should not be limited to this kind of action-oriented research. Centers should also assist in research related to determining which of the wide variety of media formats and forms of presentation can be most effective within a particular instructional unit. Comparative studies that test the value of certain types of materials in any given learning situation would help to improve media evaluation.

2. *Center governance.* Another study should analyze the governance of centers. If networks of centers are to be viable, it is essential to know which level of authority should have primary responsibility. The study should determine at which level (local, intermediate, state) centers should be administered to be most responsive to the needs of potential users and, therefore, most effective.

3. *Evaluation and networks.* A similar study would help to determine the areas of responsibility of each center in a network. If it is practical to share information, then it is possible to divide the evaluation task to be performed. The study could explore the best way to share the job, whether it is better to divide and specialize by subject or grade level or other category.

A third level of research relates to both individual centers and to those in a coordinated network. Cooperative projects, some of which could be undertaken on a pilot basis, include:

1. *Service areas.* Of vital importance is the optimum size for center service areas. A systematic plan for centers depends on knowing how far people can or will travel to examine materials, and thus the maximum area a single center can serve effectively. Shaughnessy found that "for the most part, a distance of from 10 to 15 miles (or 20 to 30 minutes travel time) marks the practical limit of central library effectiveness."[6] The study could also determine whether potential patrons would wait for materials from other centers, and how long this time period might be for various kinds of media and information. The results of such a study should provide planners with factual data to help them determine how many centers are needed and how these can relate to one another. It would also indicate whether centers might effectively share information by traditional methods, or whether they would require rapid intercommunication using more complex communication technology.

[6] Thomas Shaughnessy, "The Influence of Distance and Travel Time on Central Library Use," PhD dissertation, Rutgers, The State University (1970), p.147.

2. *Evaluation procedures.* Research into the procedures of centers is also needed. Studies should identify the criteria used in evaluating materials and the methods of securing evaluation. Center directors can improve their program if they know who should be evaluating materials and how best to organize evaluation procedures. They need to know how knowledge of the subject, grade or age level, or audience are related to competent and applicable evaluation. Whether an item can be sufficiently evaluated by applying standard criteria or whether it should be field tested may be determined by the users themselves.

3. *Selection and acquisition policies.* Centers' collections offer several opportunities for research. A study of center selection and acquisition policies would provide the basis for guidelines for selection for other centers. By studying the use of the collection over a period of time, it would also be possible to determine the optimum retention time for particular kinds of media.

PROGRAM REVIEW AND EVALUATION

Periodic review of activities and continuing evaluation of the center's progress towards its goals are significant responsibilities. This kind of review and evaluation may be a part of the center's inservice program for its own staff, but it also needs to be considered individually by members of the staff, especially by those who, as media specialists, may more frequently speak for the center and assist in the determination of its goals and the selection of its priorities.

Review and evaluation of program should precede planning for the future, but in a continuing service, the feedback from review and evaluation is so consistent that planning is not an isolated activity. Nor is it the exclusive responsibility of the director of the center. Just as others contribute to evaluation of the center's program, they should participate in planning and setting priorities for the future. The value of their participation in planning should be apparent in a number of ways, including the recognition of their own role in the center's program, their understanding of the special skills and interests of other staff members, and their ability to interpret to other groups the plans and priorities which the center has established so that they will know what action the center intends to take.

Accurate reporting of activities within the center and by the center staff is an essential component of the review and evaluation of the center. Even a simple report about talks given, demonstrations presented, evaluation committees assigned, meetings attended, and other activities undertaken may give quite a different picture of what is happening or what should be happening than is required for review, evaluation, and planning. For example, staff members may be duplicating the efforts of one another by giving demonstrations in the same school, because a principal or faculty program chairman has been particularly enthusiastic. Or, one media specialist with an enthusiastic following among the selection center's users may be getting all the opportunities for talks and demonstrations, with the result that his own work becomes too specialized and, worse yet, other specialists do not have reason to develop their own skills in this area.

Reporting of activities should be simple, requiring a minimum of time but preferably resulting in some written record. Notes of visits made to schools or other agencies, meetings attended, and consultant recommendations given by telephone or other medium should be tersely made, but in each case the media specialist reporting should include some statement (perhaps as simple as an item on a checklist) indicating whether his contribution was initiated by him, whether he was participating in response to a request, or whether his contribution was a significant aspect in support of the program, meeting, or other activity.

COMMUNICATIONS AND PUBLIC RELATIONS

The center has a clear responsibility for communicating with its several publics. Any agency or institution serving the public, especially one supported wholly or in part by public funds, must account for its operations and encourage the use of its facilities and services. The communications function of a center's total program, then, has two major elements, reporting and public relations.

1. *Reporting.*

a. The periodic financial and administrative reports may be required by the local or state governmental unit or units by which the center is sponsored and from which its funding is derived.

b. Reports of existing and projected program activities, to agencies which use the center—schools, libraries, religious and civic groups—and to other selection centers within a regional, state or national network. These reports should cover collections (with particular reference to the addition of actual new media or their evaluations in specialized subjects or for certain grade levels), facilities, inservice instructional opportunities, special services, and personnel changes.

c. A selective dissemination of information system for individual users known to be interested in particular disciplines, subjects, kinds of media, or levels of use, e.g., preschool materials. Such a system is especially important for teachers and media specialists and will vary according to the level of the center.

d. Since communications implies a two-way street, user interests should be determined by a user survey which has the additional value of providing the kinds of data required for planning the nature and scope of the center's collections and its training programs. An initial user survey, conducted before the center becomes operational, is an essential element of program planning. Subsequent user surveys should be undertaken periodically, possibly on an annual basis, to reveal changing needs and use patterns. An annual survey also reinforces budget requests submitted to the sponsoring municipal or state education agencies.

2. *Public relations.* In concept and application, a public relations program involves far more than sending publicity releases to newspapers and radio and television stations. It has, in fact, been called "the engineering of consent," i.e., attracting and maintaining the favorable opinion, participation, and continuing support of an agency's several constituencies.

A media selection center should design a continuing information program aimed principally to reach and involve a professional public and, secondarily, the wider community. Procedures and techniques vary in some respects from customary publicity practices.

Informing and involving the professional users within a center's immediate area of service, and keeping other centers informed about the collection, evaluations, inservice training, and related programs require, however, an intimate knowledge of what classroom teachers, media specialists, curriculum specialists, school administrators, and other potential users need and want to know, and the ability to convey that information in a useful and compelling way.

Here are some of the elements of a public relations and information program:

a. For the professional audience:

i. A mailing list of individuals, teachers, librarians, and others who are actual or potential users of the center at the local level or who have some direct or indirect local responsibility for its governance. This list should be keyed for selective dissemination of information and must be constantly updated.

ii. A mailing list of individuals who may have less immediate concern, involvement, and responsibility but who should be kept informed, e.g., directors of other centers, senior staff members of the state department of education and the state library agency, deans of schools of library service and of teacher training institutions outside of the center's normal service area.

iii. A basic descriptive brochure which explains the center's purposes, governance, programs, and services.

iv. A monthly bulletin or newsletter reporting new acquisitions and evaluations, inservice instructional plans; staff-written or contributed features on new forms of educational media and their use, the results of center-sponsored research, and personnel changes.

v. Active participation by the director and senior staff of the center in professional conferences, institutes, and seminars where the center's program can be explained.

vi. Periodic special exhibits and demonstrations of all kinds of media. The dissemination of information about evaluations and about inservice instructional programs is especially important. Centers created at the state level to serve a network should consider the development of publications in these two fields to coordinate information developed at the local level and to make it available efficiently and rapidly.

b. For the community:

i. Development of a basic list of publicity outlets, including the publications of community service organizations.

ii. Distribution to this list of news releases about the formation, staff, programs, and expansion of the center, with emphasis on its ultimate purpose and role in the improvement of education in the community, region or state, and benefits to children, young adults, and adults.

iii. Invitations to public officials, civic leaders, and the press to attend special exhibits and demonstrations.

iv. Talks by the center director and senior staff to program or general meetings of those civic, religious, labor, or other private voluntary agencies, organizations, and clubs which sponsor and conduct youth-serving informal educational activities and projects.

Regional and state-level centers can apply similar procedures, once the nature and scope of their professional and public constituencies have been defined. But in the end, the way in which professionals and the public view the center and use its facilities ultimately depends not on what it says, but on what it does, on its performance and on the ways in which staff members respond to requests from users. A churlish or careless reply to even the most naïve telephone inquiry can wreck the most thoughtfully planned and executed public information program.

5

Media Collections

The collection of materials in an educational media selection center includes resources for evaluation, examination, and selection for use in preschool through young adult and special education programs. It contains current media and retrospective materials in various formats, determined principally by the needs of the clientele within the center's service area.

Many collections identified in Phase I were allowed to grow by accretion of gifts of sample copies or demonstration models from publishers and producers, with budgeted aquisitions provided on an erratic or minimal basis. Thus, media not worth the time to examine have accumulated in some collections, and in many others, materials pertinent to the purposes of the center or agencies served are missing, primarily because they could not be or were not acquired through publisher/producer largesse.

To build and maintain an effective selection and examination center collection, therefore, it is essential to spell out its purposes and parameters, and to allocate an adequate budget for acquiring materials on the basis of such factors as:

1. The goals and functions of the center
2. The nature and needs of the constituent groups to be served, existing and projected, as determined by user surveys
3. The range and scope of holdings required to meet these needs, planned if necessary, in stages
4. The accessibility of the holdings and resources of other media selection centers in the same area, or network
5. The policies for selection which reflect these needs, purposes, and functions
6. The adequacy of funding.

It is particularly important that plans for the center's collection be predicated upon the assumption that there will eventually be a network in which the individual center will have its place and role. This constitutes a further reason and force for requiring planners to consider carefully at this point the limitations of the collection and its relationship to other possible centers in a network. For example, only the National Laboratory System projected in chapter 9 can conceivably afford to build an exhaustive or even a comprehensive collection in a wide variety of subjects or interest levels. A regional or state center, however, can work towards comprehensiveness and will have fewer limitations than a local or district center. Limits may appropriately be set at the parameter of media for specific grade levels (from elementary grades at one end of the scale to media used with adult illiterates and new literates at the other) or for special needs (black studies, exceptional children, Indian culture). Planners of collections in such special areas should recognize, however, that many general media can be used in special ways. Limiting collections to books and printed materials alone is not realistic in the light of the educational needs of the times. An initial focus might, however, be indicated for the acquisition of *current* media.

Center planners should be aware that a media selection center must do more than simply "recognize" both print and audiovisual materials. In fact, the Phase I report emphasizes that the success of educational media centers will require strong directors who embrace both print and audiovisual concepts.[1]

RETROSPECTIVE COLLECTION

Those media necessary for comparative evaluation to support the selection and evaluation functions of the center and to provide backup for the advisory and instructional work of the center will form the retrospective collection. This collection will represent a considerable investment over a period of time but will provide the backbone of the expanding services of a truly effective center. In some respects this collection may appear to duplicate the curriculum materials in a college or university or a "standard" collection for the elementary or high school library. It will be constantly enriched by the best of the material from the current collection, and it should be constantly weeded for outdated or no longer relevant materials. Major portions of the retrospective collection should consist of:

1. A full range of print and audiovisual materials, fiction and nonfiction, for those age levels and subject specialists determined by policy for the collection of the center, with constant reviewing to achieve the center's goals.

[1] Rowell and Heidbreder, p.79–81.

2. Relevant dictionaries, encyclopedias, newspapers, and periodicals, as well as textbooks, both basal and supplementary, used in the schools in the geographical area served. For example, in a district center, users should be able to find the latest editions of the best encyclopedias and other reference sets for examination prior to purchase. Some general educational materials, including journals, could be added to the retrospective collection if the planners determine that they are essential to the center's users. A regional or state center, and certainly the National Laboratory System, would be responsible for having collections in all these categories.

3. Professional materials, including periodicals that serve the evaluation and selection functions; reports on new programs for the use of media in teaching and learning; and professional publications about organization of media collections.

4. Collections of trade and national bibliographies and selection aids, such as *Cumulative Book Index*, the latest issues of NICEM indexes (the series published by the National Information Center for Educational Media, University of Southern California), *Publisher's Trade List Annual, Publishers Weekly, Landers Film Review, Booklist, Audiovisual Market Place, Books in Print, Westinghouse Learning Directory, Literary Market Place*, Educator's Progress Service bibliographies, and a subscription to the National Catalog Service of the Library of Congress and to general evaluative lists such as the Wilson Catalog series.

5. A comprehensive collection of current publishers', producers', and wholesalers' catalogs of books, audiovisual materials and equipment; announcements of governmental bibliographies, manuals, and document source references; curriculum publications issued both by the state and the community; indexes of community resources; releases about local, state, and national teachers' meetings; local, state and national television and radio program guides; supplemental adult-education program brochures for workshops and seminars.

One of the means by which planners can best limit their objectives, and therefore the functions and collection of the center, is to face at once the expense of maintaining an adequate retrospective collection made up of the components listed above. These elements constitute the tools by which current new materials can be identified and acquired and from which substantive guidance will be secured for the users of the center in evaluating materials. They also constitute sources and tools which will be continuously needed for reference and use by the center staff. The comparison of new media with older, already available media is an essential part of the evaluation process, and it is impossible to carry out comparative evaluation without an adequate retrospective collection, at least of the basic, standard titles. Determining limitations of the retrospective collection, therefore, is a useful preliminary exercise in the determination of the center's overall objectives and scope.

CURRENT COLLECTION

Procedures are also established whereby print and nonprint media are secured for examination and evaluation on a current and continuing basis. The materials are requested for reviewing and previewing purposes with the understanding that those found desirable for further evaluation or other use will be purchased; the others, returned in good condition. The length of borrowing time before they are purchased is determined between the center and the supplier.

Where local policy permits, arrangements may be made with selected publishers, producers, or wholesalers for automatic delivery of print and audiovisual materials as they are published or produced. Some wholesalers, for example, have already developed thesauri or categorized "profiles" by which a buyer can indicate the subjects and subdivisions, the grade levels, and the depths in collecting of materials wanted for automatic, on approval delivery. As center staffs begin to function in this way, it seems probable that enterprising wholesalers will develop, in collaboration with professionals, thesauri and profiles based on the characteristics of elementary and secondary educational media centers, like those that exist for college and university libraries.

If, on the other hand, local regulations restrict or do not permit approval ordering, the center must set up an elaborate system for checking announcements, publishers' and producers' catalogs, current bibliographies of all kinds of media, and the like. Some checking of this kind is needed, of course, even when materials are ordered on approval.

The normal length of time for retaining current purchased materials in the center is from eighteen to twenty-four months. The staff of the center then decides what to retain in the retrospective collection on the basis of the selection policies previously determined for it.

ACQUISITION OF MATERIALS

Centers should budget for the purchase of all media in their collections for a number of valid reasons. When a center depends only on free contributions of media, its collection is incomplete and inadequate. When all media in a given area are available for evaluation, comparison of one with another is possible, and a valid selection can be made in terms of which is better for what purpose and which user.

A collection in which one medium is emphasized more than another fails to meet the objectives set forth for an educational media center of any kind today. The availability in an examination center of slides, art prints, realia, books, films and auditory records in the form of tapes, recordings, or educational television, has opened an infinite variety of possibilities for more effective learning and, therefore, of materials needed by the teacher and other educational workers.

Types of media which may be included are listed below. The list will change as new products are marketed.

Books: hardcover and paperback, trade and textbooks with components
Magazines: a selected group of children's, professional, trade and popular
Newspapers: local, state, national, and foreign languages as appropriate
Pamphlets
Curriculum guides
8mm film loops
16mm films
Filmstrips
Tape and disc recordings
Transparencies
Graphic materials: art prints (reproductions), charts, pictures, and study prints
Globes
Maps
Microforms: card, fiche, and film
Programmed instructional materials
Multimedia kits
Art objects
Videotape recordings
Realia: models, dioramas, replicas, etc.
Kinescopes
Toys and games
Simulation media

When the center collection is being established, a first step is to start securing current collections and at the same time to begin to build a retrospective core collection. From this point on it is a matter of retaining as a core those materials which have been favorably evaluated and withdrawing those which have become obsolete. The aim is to establish a retrospective collection that supports the highest standards for media collections in all agencies served. Therefore, the local selection center might have current

50

books by outstanding and popular authors and maintain in the retrospective collection only a small, representative selection of these works, while the regional or national selection center, or libraries serving the general public, could have most or all of the older titles.

ORGANIZATION OF COLLECTIONS

In organization, the retrospective collection reflects best current practices in cataloging, classification, and processing. It demonstrates good methods, allowing also for experimentation. The use of the Dewey Decimal Classification is recommended as the one most likely to be used by professional and nonprofessional users. One assumes that any use of machine-readable cataloging (MARC) or other automated systems will be compatible with Dewey. Since July 1971 the Library of Congress and book publishers have cooperated in the important Cataloging in Publication (CIP) Program, providing cataloging data in the books that include both Dewey and Library of Congress classification numbers.

Cataloging procedures for print and nonprint materials should be based upon national standards as recommended by the American Library Association and the Association of Educational Communications and Technology. The use of commercial or cooperative processing should be explored, so that professional staff time need not be dissipated in technical processing of the retrospective collection, and so that access will be quick and economical. Newly established centers should consider the feasibility of such processes as keypunching, book catalogs, and the like. One or two examples now exist where contracts have been made between two agencies for the establishment of a selection center, with one providing space, staff, and materials and the other providing technical services. In such an arrangement it is possible that no exchange of funds is necessary, only an exchange of services.

In some instances, current media may remain uncataloged or be temporarily recorded until they have gone through the complete routine of screening, evaluation, and field testing. At the completion of this process, the materials retained for the current collection are organized by subject and subdivided within the broad subject.

A simplified, but not necessarily complete, record is kept with at least five points of access: author, title, subject, format, and producer/publisher. A coding system for identification and location (*perhaps* based on Dewey Decimal Classification) is devised in which broad subject areas, sub-subject areas, recommended grade level, and evaluation are noted. A combination of symbols and numbers permits flexibility. The plan of organization

51

adopted must be flexible enough to allow for unlimited numbers and kinds of materials. Centers should take all possible advantage of International Standard Book Numbers (ISBN), International Standard Serial Numbers (ISSN), and other standard numbering systems as they are developed.

HOUSING OF COLLECTIONS

For effective use of the total collection, it should be divided into current and retrospective materials. Within both the retrospective and current collections, trade books and audiovisual materials may be intershelved. Textbooks, both retrospective and current, are shelved as a unit under broad subject headings, subdivided by levels: elementary, junior high, senior high, and adult.

Each center houses the audiovisual equipment necessary for demonstration but not lending purposes. There should be enough equipment to ensure that all forms of media can be viewed, projected or heard, and evaluated. The center has a collateral responsibility to assist in equipment selection. As rapid changes in technology apply to both audiovisual media and the accompanying equipment, correlation between materials and equipment is a prime consideration on a continuing basis. When an educational media selection center is set up, it should have at least one of each piece (preferably different manufacturers for two or more) of the following listed equipment:

Film projectors: 16mm and 8mm
2″ x 2″ slide projectors
Filmstrip or combination filmstrip-slide projectors
Sound filmstrip projectors
Overhead projectors
Opaque projectors
Filmstrip viewers
Stereoscopic and microscope slide viewers
Microprojectors
Polarized attachments for slide and transparency projectors
Record player with junction box and 8 to 10 headsets
Audiotape recorders
Listening station
Projection carts
Projection screen: sizes 18″ x 18″ table type, 60″ and 70″ tripod and
   wall

Photocopying machine
Duplicating machine
Microreader, some with microfiche attachment
Microreader printer
Portable videotape recorder system with monitor
Film inspection and repair equipment.

Each center should also keep a small supply of replacements, such as bulbs, spools, electrical cords, threeway switches, adaptors, blank tapes, inks, transparencies (flat and rolls), etc., and repair supplies.

6

Center Personnel Tasks

Since the functions of a center are associated with the collection and use of the media housed there and the educational needs of the center's users; and since some are the kinds of tasks which must be conducted in any agency where policies, budgets, planning and administration are integral to daily operations, the tasks to be performed are grouped here according to these different categories, rather than according to the level or type of personnel responsible for them.[1] In centers where the staff consists only of one or two persons, each member may conduct some of the work in each category. In centers where size and functions allow for the use of a number of experts on a part-time or on-call basis, some of these tasks may be performed by persons other than the permanent staff employed by the center. And, in some instances, the special location and audience of the center may require tasks much more complex than those noted here.

This list relies, in part, on "Checklist of Duties," included in *Task Analysis Survey Instrument* published by the American Library Association, School Library Manpower Project, in 1969. A number of the tasks are described exactly as they appear there; others have been recast in terms of the work of media selection centers; still others have been added.

For administrative consistency and clarity, these tasks must be performed in the center:

1. Determine policies in consultation with the user and supporting agencies.
2. Plan operations and maintenance.
3. Confer with advisers and administrators concerning operations, programs, and budgets.

---

[1] It should be noted that, in this arrangement, some tasks overlap: i.e., providing information and other services to cooperating agencies and individual users; maintaining evaluation and other files.

4. Evaluate, select, obtain, and maintain retrospective and current collections of media.
5. Determine budget needs.
6. Record income and expenditures for the center.
7. Maintain photographic, audio, and textual records.
8. Plan arrangement of space and furniture.
9. Schedule use of facilities.
10. Prepare job descriptions for the staff.
11. Prepare and maintain procedural manual for the staff.
12. Assign duties and work schedules to the staff.
13. Select personnel for employment in the center.
14. Conduct instructional programs and other meetings for the staff of the center.
15. Route selection tools, periodicals, bulletins, etc., to the center staff.
16. Interpret administrative regulations and directions which may affect the staff.
17. Supervise and evaluate the work of the staff.

Effective use of the media located in the center and of the full resources of the faculty requires that the following tasks be performed:

1. Schedule assignment of media, staff, and facilities.
2. Prepare and distribute necessary operational forms.
3. Determine records and statistics needed for operation.
4. Compile and tabulate data for statistical reports.
5. Engage in research activities related to media and their utilization.
6. Submit reports to persons and groups responsible for the center's program.
7. Design and produce media as needed for the program.
8. Write and edit news articles, promotional materials, and notices about the center for local newspapers and other media.
9. Maintain publicity records.
10. Plan and implement proposals for more effective programs in the center.
11. Work cooperatively with other selection centers and with other media agencies.

To ensure that the media located in the center are as accessible and as useful as possible, the staff should:

1. Establish and maintain efficient arrangement of media.
2. Maintain a full range of aids for selection of media.

3. Maintain and use, for quick reference, a collection of tools to expedite selection, examination, and use of media.
4. Read evaluation reports, review media, publishers' catalogs, jobbers' lists, producers' notes, etc., to determine which media should be obtained by the center.
5. Confer with representatives of media producers and suppliers.
6. Maintain records of media requested, housed temporarily or permanently in the center, and/or loaned or sent out for preview or evaluation.
7. Determine policy for acceptance and use of gift media, catalogs, promotional materials, etc.
8. Acknowledge gift media.
9. Seek and follow through on suggestions of media to be examined.
10. Evaluate media for location in the center.
11. Plan and implement evaluation of media for specific purposes and audiences.
12. Plan and implement the disposal of media after their examination period.
13. Inspect media on a regular schedule for possible damage or wear.
14. Evaluate, select, obtain, and maintain appropriate equipment for examination or demonstration of materials.
15. Perform simple repair work as needed on media.
16. Arrange for major repair or replacement of media as needed.

As a service agency which receives support and assistance from other agencies in its community as well as from suppliers and producers, the center must relate to these outside agencies. Among some of the tasks to be performed are:

1. Conduct necessary correspondence.
2. Attend and participate at meetings of professional organizations.
3. Maintain files of correspondence, requisitions, requests and orders for media, supplies, and other needs.
4. Check lists and bibliographies to determine whether media included are, have been, or should be in the center.
5. Compile and distribute such items as lists of media new to the center, lists of programs and services offered by the center, etc.
6. Perform delivery service of media for review, of media loaned by other agencies, etc.
7. Select, order, inventory, and maintain supplies.
8. Prepare and distribute notices, requisitions, bulletins, bibliographies, buying guides, letters stencils, orders.

9. Visit schools, libraries, and other agencies where actual and potential users of the center may be located.

These responsibilities are a part of the center's program of direct service to actual and potential users:

1. Conduct tours of the facility.
2. Assist users in locating media.
3. Maintain file of information on how to use equipment.
4. Provide materials for and assist users in production of legal photocopies, notes on media examined, etc., as requested.
5. Prepare for projection and, when necessary, project media requested by users.
6. Assist and encourage individuals to use the facility and services of the center.
7. Conduct, or assist in conducting, programs for groups using the facility and its media.
8. Assist committees or other groups in selecting media for specific purposes.
9. Compile information on actual and potential users to provide for their special interests and needs.

For the full potential of the center to be realized, these tasks need to be performed to promote and extend its program:

1. Plan talks and media presentations, etc., to familiarize groups with the program.
2. Participate in curricular planning which has implications for use of the center.
3. Arrange and conduct workshops and instructional sessions on preview, evaluation, and selection of media.
4. Maintain files of users' evaluations and reactions, and reviewers of specific media.
5. Conduct and participate in workshops on techniques of media production.

In planning the operations of even a small center, virtually all of these tasks must be allocated in a table of organization. At the outset the minimum staff should be:

2 fulltime professionals, the director and a media specialist
1 general media assistant

1 media technician
1 administrative assistant
3 clerk-typists
1 custodian

7

Facilities

Since an educational media selection center, in terms of the clientele, collection, instruction, methodology, and administrative procedures evolves as our society evolves educationally, technologically, and demographically, the physical facility for such a center should be as capable of change as the program it serves. No guidelines can indicate all of the possible combinations of variables for any one center in response to its needs, its resources, and its state and rate of technological and philosophical development. The process of planning a facility involves asking a number of questions, postulating alternative answers, choosing the most efficient alternative in terms of effectiveness and economy, and, finally, doing the careful calculations which provide guidance for the architect who is involved with other professional planners.

QUESTIONS TO BE ANSWERED OR CONSIDERED

I. What are the functions of the educational media selection center? What activities are anticipated?
   A. Housing a multimedia collection of materials and equipment
      1. How many of each type of printed and audiovisual media will be housed?
      2. What can or will be in reduced photographic form?
      3. How many and what kinds of equipment are needed for listening, reviewing, and producing hardcopy from photographic forms?
      4. Will all materials and equipment be available for examination on open shelves in the main area? If not, what provision needs to be made for additional stack or storage area?

5. Will there be separate resource rooms or areas for collections in some disciplines or subjects?
6. Will the collection be organized by format of materials, subject, level of use, or a combination of these? What are the special housing requirements for various formats? Shelving, files, temperature, and access are among these requirements.
7. What provision will be made for the evaluation of programs for cable television?

B. Identifying and locating resources
1. What keys to the collection will be provided? What are the space and furniture requirements for them?
2. Has consideration been given to the advantages and disadvantages of book versus card catalogs in terms of space and furnishing requirements, ease of preparation and maintenance, and convenient use?

C. Viewing, listening, reading, writing, inservice workshops, conferences
1. How many clients should be accommodated at one time? For what kinds of activities?
2. How many large-group spaces are needed and for what kinds of use—film showings, telelectures, other presentations?
3. How many small-group spaces are needed for use by selection committees, workshops, demonstrations?
4. How many individual spaces are needed at tables, carrels, microreaders, and in lounge areas?
5. Are there sufficient electrical outlets with provision for changing, adding, and relocating them as the need arises? Is needed electrical power available?
6. What flexibility can be built in to cope with new media such as video-playback systems? Can kits or packages of multimedia materials be used conveniently at one station?

D. Administration of center
1. How many professional staff members are needed?
2. How many nonprofessional staff members are needed?
3. How much space should be allowed for desks, file cabinets, coat racks?
4. Will a lounge area for staff be provided?
5. How many telephones are required?

E. Acquisition and processing
1. What are the space needs if all acquisition and processing are done on the premises, if processing is done commercially or by a regional center; if acquisition procedures are computerized?

2. Is the receiving area for new materials adequate in terms of size and convenience?

F. Display and exhibit
1. What are the space needs for special collections, for commercial exhibits, for vertical display areas and units?

G. Limited circulation
1. What kinds and quantities of material will circulate, if any?
2. What special charge-out and return provisions are needed?
3. Do special carrying cases and storage for materials need to be provided?

H. Individual consultation
1. Are special conference rooms required or can small group areas or offices be used for this purpose?

I. Publication and duplication
1. Will dissemination activities include printing, photocopying, mimeographing, telecommunications, computer terminals?
2. What are the space requirements for preparation, supplies, equipment, mailing?

J. Simple maintenance and repair of equipment
1. What are the space requirements for storage of simple parts and tools—bulbs, tubes, extension wires, testing devices?
2. How much work space is needed?

K. Mobile services
1. If mobile services are to be provided, what are the space, heat, and light requirements for housing the unit?
2. What factors must be considered for ease of stocking and unloading: e.g., loading area on same level as collection, storage space for carts and hand trucks to move materials?

II. What auxiliary services will the center provide for its users?
A. Restroom facilities
B. Public telephones
C. Typing room
D. Food services
1. Coffee- and/or food-dispensing machines
2. Coffee preparation facilities—storage for ingredients and utensils, sink, hot plate or stove
3. Refrigeration
E. Coat racks

III. What environmental factors need to be considered?
A. Light

1. To what extent should natural daylight be utilized?
2. What variation in lighting should be provided for day and evening?
3. What are the light requirements for reading, writing, various kinds of viewing?
4. Has glare from windows been considered and dealt with?
B. Temperature and ventilation
1. What type of heating system is most efficient for the climate?
2. What are the air conditioning and dehumidification requirements?
3. What provision has been made for adequate ventilation?
C. Mobility
1. Has adequate provision been made to allow for ease of movement of users? Do traffic patterns follow the natural flow of people to and from collections, utilization and study areas?
2. Have ramps and other provisions been made for the physically handicapped?
D. Sound
1. What provision has been made for acoustical treatment of floors, ceilings, or special areas, such as music listening rooms, typing rooms, offices, etc.?
2. Has the layout been planned to separate inherently noisy areas from quiet areas?
E. Color
1. Does the color scheme create a pleasant environment; creative but not distracting, comfortable but not monotonous?
F. Furnishings
1. Are furnishings attractive and appropriate to their function? Do they create an inviting atmosphere?

IV. What factors need to be considered in site selection?
A. General location
1. Will the center primarily serve an urban, geographically contained population or a widely dispersed rural or suburban population?
2. Is public transportation readily available?
3. Is adequate automobile parking space provided?
4. Has careful consideration been given to the advantages and disadvantages of locating near cultural or commercial centers for convenient access versus building in a more remote location where land may be cheaper?
5. Are neighboring enterprises nondistracting in terms of noise and general aesthetics?

6. Are essential services available—trash and snow removal, water, sewage, electricity, fire and police protection?

When these questions have been carefully considered and the basic decisions made, specifications for furnishings and layout can be made. The need for flexibility cannot be overemphasized. Regardless of the existing and immediately predictable functions of the educational media center, they are subject to change as education changes and as new forms of communication are developed and become readily available. Assistance in planning a specific layout is available through publications listed in the bibliography, from commercial suppliers, and, of course, from the architect.

8

Budgeting

Budgeting for a center requires, first, careful analysis of its purposes, program, media, and facilities. Although such an analysis would not produce a cost-benefit program because of the intangible nature of the projected effects, the planning group responsible for the fiscal aspects of a new or augmented center needs these data.

If a local, regional, or state-level center is being established with no pre-existing physical facilities, planners must deal first with design, construction, and nonrecurring equipment costs. Ideally, the initial local, state, or federal appropriation for capital expenses should provide for the full range of facilities identified in chapter 7. Estimates of actual construction and annual operating costs cannot be spelled out here because of the geographical, administrative, and program variables. However, installation costs and annual expenses for the examination center in Harrisburg, Pennsylvania, are shown in appendix 2.

The application of the principles of program budgeting can ensure the gradual development of centers, with funding assigned to identified needs so that the center and its program will continue to be versatile and dynamic.

In his book, *Educational Planning-Programming-Budgeting*,[1] Harry J. Hartley lists as essentials in program budgeting the formulation of a philosophy, goals, and specific objective; a determination of personnel, space, and materials requirements; the establishing of priorities; an analysis of financial resources available; and a consistent review and evaluation process to demonstrate how specific objectives are being met and to design alternative means of achieving these objectives. He suggests three time spans for planning and budgeting.

1. Long-range plans: at least five years, perhaps longer
2. Medium-range plans: three to five years
3. Short-range plan: the immediate year.

[1] Englewood Cliffs, N. J.: Prentice-Hall, 1968.

64

Any agency contemplating the establishment of a selection center should proceed accordingly. Once a conceptual determination has been made, planning can begin for each time span. No single realistic budget can be suggested which fits all situations because of the variations of possible services, of the size and scope of the collections, and of the variety in possible administrative patterns and salary differentials. There are, however, basic components which must be budgeted for regardless of the scope of the program or the stage of its development. These are:

1. *Facilities.* New or additional construction, necessary renovations, and rent; spatial growth and technological changes as related to program development and the expansion of collections of materials and equipment; possible expansion of the facility and site originally selected.

2. *Personnel.* Salaries and benefits for the director and other professional staff persons; permanent administrative, clerical, and custodial positions; consultant fees.

3. *Administration and operations.* Rent (where applicable); interest (when chargeable); maintenance and security; fuel; insurance; utilities (sufficient to allow for frequent or prolonged use of audiovisual, xerographic, and other reproductive equipment); expendable supplies; staff travel; and communications (allowing for sophisticated electronic means of information transfer where available). Operational costs will, in general, be increased as the center's hours or program of service are extended.

4. *Materials and equipment.* A schedule of priorities (short, medium, and long range) should be established for the purchase of materials and for the purchase and (in some instances, rental) of the equipment required for their demonstration.

5. *Evaluation and instructional activities.* The costs of all evaluation services, and of inservice or other instruction provided for any group, including the center staff. Specific cost items may include: reimbursement of participants' travel expenses and fees for substitute teachers—if and as required; fees or honoraria and travel expenses for outside evaluators; production costs of the expendable special materials, forms, bulletins, etc., used either in the evaluation process or in training and public information programs; and the direct expenses, other than fees, incurred for conferences and workshops sponsored by the center.

BUDGET PREPARATION

Burton Friedman suggests that an actual budget be prepared in such a manner that the cost of each substantive activity can be determined. He recommends the use of cost centers to record all costs of a function.[2] Functions can be divided into the following categories and each assigned a cost center number:

1. Administration   Cost center 284
2. Selection and Acquisition of Materials and
    Equipment   Cost center 285 (table 2)
3. Evaluation and Instructional Activities   Cost center 286
4. Dissemination   Cost center 287
5. Research   Cost center 288

Dissemination and Research are shown as separate functions because they are concerned with the total program rather than any one aspect of it.

If Mr. Friedman's suggestion is followed, rent, utilities, and maintenance would appear in the budget for each cost center; the amount budgeted for each would represent a prorated share of the space assigned to each function and the length of time the assigned space is used. Other items which appear in each cost center budget include salaries, social security, retirement, postage, and supplies.

SOURCES OF FUNDS

Funding a comprehensive educational media selection center is expensive. Few small school districts can afford it, and there has been little evidence thus far that many centers have been adequately supported on the kind of continuing basis required for the development of a fully effective program. Federal revenue-sharing plans implemented in 1973 could well affect state and local center funding. All appropriate efforts must be made to secure some of these funds for center support.

Sources include local public funds provided at the discretion of the board of education, or other institutions in some instances, as part of a bond issue for the expansion of education facilities in the community; the appropriation of state and federal funds; and combinations of public and private funds where, for example, a privately supported institution of higher education becomes the sponsoring agency. Federal funds may be made available under existing educational funding programs, particularly if the center is sponsored and supported cooperatively by a consortium of, for example, a school district, a public library system, and a local teacher-training institution.

[2] *Program-Oriented Information: A Management Systems Complex for State Education Agencies.* Part 1: Analysis and Proposals (Baltimore, Md.: State Department of Education, 1961).

Table 2. BUDGET FORMAT FOR ONE COST CENTER

Unit EMSC	Cost Center 285 Selection and Acquisition	Source of Funds	Amount (in dollars)
	Salaries	000	$
	Retirement	000	
	Social Security	000	
	Included here are salaries and benefits for all persons involved in the selection, acquisition and organization of materials and equipment.		
	Rent ⎫	000	
	Maintenance ⎬ all prorated	000	
	Utilities ⎭	000	
	Printed materials	001[a]	
	Audiovisual materials	001	
	A-V equipment 50/50	000–001	
	Supplies	000	
	Postage and other communication costs	000	
	Printing	000–001	
	Travel	000	
	Transportation	000	
	Consultant (to advise on organization of center)	000–001	
	Special furniture and equipment	000	
	Contractual service: repair and upkeep of machines	000	

[a] "001" to designate state or federal funds, if available.

9

Networks

The increasing volume and variety of media being produced and the growing complexity and rapidity of change in education make it impossible for even the largest of media centers alone to gather, evaluate, select, and organize for use all appropriate media in a reasonable time.

Media centers must, therefore, become linked, as are other organizations in education and government, in such cooperative arrangements as consortia, centralized data and technical processing systems, joint acquisitions and reference services programs, and other similar activities. These arrangements, coupled with communications capabilities, are today referred to as networks.

Networking is a rapidly advancing concept in information services. By definition a network is "an interconnection of things, systems, or organizations."[1]

An ideal network displays four characteristics:

a. *Formal Organization*
Many units sharing a common information purpose recognize the value of group affiliation and enter into a compact.

b. *Communications*
The network includes circuits that rapidly interconnect dispersed points.

c. *Bi-directional Operation*
Information may move in either direction, and provision is made for each network participant to send as well as receive.

d. *A Directory and Switching Capability*
A directory look-up system enables a participant to identify the

---

[1] Joseph Becker and Wallace C. Olsen, "Information Networks," in *Annual Review of Information Science and Technology,* ed. by Carlos Cuadra (Chicago: Encyclopaedia Britannica, 1968), p.288.

unit most able to satisfy a particular request. A switching center then routes messages to the unit over the optimum communications path.[2]

These capabilities need not always depend on unfamiliar, difficult-to-use advanced technology. The telephone system contains circuits that can be rapidly connected and provide bidirectional operation. One network development in education is simply a closed-circuit television channel carrying the teacher to a group of students, and an open telephone circuit arranged to conduct a regular conference call to allow students in different locations and the teacher to talk back and forth while the lecture is in progress. A librarian or a teacher who directs students to specific collections in a library, or to reference books on different shelves, is performing a directory task; and when one refers the student to another library, or to another teacher, one is performing a switching function. One performs that function also when he makes a series of telephone calls on behalf of a student in order to bring him into contact with an information source.

A prime impetus for the growing phenomenon of networks is the rapid and dramatic advance in communications technology which provides more kinds of channels to transmit more kinds of messages and signals farther, more rapidly, and even more cheaply than ever before. Hence, the modern media selection center should not only be prepared to work with other agencies to fill its users' needs, but it should also plan to introduce and use several different electronic communications facilities to achieve access to other parts of the system. The teletype machine, the touch-tone telephone, the computer terminal with a TV-type screen and a typewriter-like keyboard, and a facsimile scanner and receiver should be normal equipment for a media selection center. Advanced centers will have film chains for television viewing of motion pictures, radio transmitters, and receivers, television cameras, and other electronic equipment.

LEVELS OF NETWORKING FOR SELECTION

Two levels of networking are important in media selection center operation. First, centers should be involved in networks at the local, regional, and state levels. They can join or tap other local networks and form networks among themselves. It is imperative that this development at the local level be encouraged since it is here that the unique or peculiar concerns of communities can best be addressed. Furthermore, it is at this local level

[2] Ibid., p.290–91.

that programs and their funding can be made most viable. Large-scale national networks are subject to changes, including cancellation, for administrative and political reasons that may be unrelated to local needs. National networks take longer to form, generally cannot respond in the detail or the breadth of service required at the local level, and may involve serious jurisdictional questions that could preclude full service in some locales.

Local networks can get underway with simple agreements, perhaps to share resources, to cooperate in joint acquisitions programs, or to offer unique services region-wide. Local communications costs are cheaper, hence easier to handle in a network service. It is most likely, as a matter of fact, that the soundest national network of media selection centers will ultimately be developed and made successful as an extension, or an inter-communications linking, of regional networks, thereby forming a national grid.

Second, a national program of selection and evaluation should be designed to cast a wide net over producers of media, with a sufficient number of specialists monitoring the market in their areas of expertise to ensure coverage of all subjects of interest. Through coordination of ongoing acquisition, selection, and evaluation programs, the addition of new ones to fill gaps, and the provision of long-distance communications trunks, a national system should increase the quantity of media reviewed and made accessible and, at the same time, should tend to reduce unnecessary duplication of services and collections. A high degree of such duplication is inevitable in an uncoordinated regional network.

Networking at the Local Level. Networking for cooperation at the local level is essential in the face of the pressures of economy and time. It is the most effective way to use local funds for library and other media services. There are several models for local networking. Many states have communication networks linking libraries of various kinds to the state libraries by telephone (WATS [Wide-Area Telephone Service] for economy) or by TWX (Teletypewriter Exchange Service), whereby printed messages are delivered.

Organizations have been established to perform centralized technical processing functions, such as the Ohio College Library Center and the now-defunct ANYLTS, Association of New York Libraries for Technical Services. The chief products of these processing centers are book orders and catalog copy, provided for participating libraries at lower costs than they might have to pay if working independently. Properly organized, these centralized services can operate union catalog services to locate material in member libraries as a by-product of technical services. Union catalog services are essential in systems that share resources.

70

Such processing centers supply materials to libraries and provide local cataloging copy. These are effective and useful functions, but many educational agencies have additional needs that call for a wider range of communications capabilities. Many schools share classroom experiences. Frequently they must extend limited media resources to a wide range of students, geographically dispersed. Emphasis is being given to nearly instantaneous access to media tailored to individual student's requirements from remote files. All·of these needs relate to the media selection process; networks formed for other purposes can thus be useful in realizing the EMSC concept.

Increasingly the educational community is turning to the new and rapidly developing electronic communications technology to bring the full power of media to bear on local problems. All of the electronic capabilities now used in school media centers for in-house services, such as dial-access and closed-circuit television viewing, can be extended to provide similar access to the media from a regional or remote center. The costs for such communications, of course, will rise, sometimes rather rapidly, depending upon the number of channels required, the distance and time required for transmission, and the quality of signal required. While not all communications capabilities everywhere are available for use, the move to upgrade local facilities and channels is inexorable.

Some Electronic Capabilities for Local Use. The telephone, of course, is ubiquitous. With it a local center can provide not only voice communications with other centers for the exchange of information about media, but it can also transmit facsimile pictures of printed materials and communicate with computers to query for information about media stored in their magnetic memories. Almost as widespread are the teletype capabilities that allow for the transmission of typed messages.

Special microwave channels are being built in competition with the large telephone systems (e.g., Bell and General Telephone) especially for the transmission of data among computers and for video signals. An entirely new, nationwide system for data transmission, including not only microwave but also wire and satellite facilities with newly invented video switching equipment, is under construction.[3] These newly authorized facilities will soon increase the speed and variety of communications among libraries and similar agencies.

Cable television (CATV), too, is spreading rapidly throughout the nation, increasing quite dramatically the channel capacity for transmission

---

[3] The facilities herein referred to are being constructed by Microwave Communications Incorporated and DATRAN, just two of a number of firms entering the industry.

of video signals. Many communities require licenses to allocate a significant portion of CATV capacity for educational purposes. Before too long it should be possible for media centers in many cities to use these channels almost as freely and easily as they use telephones. The investment in terminal equipment will naturally be higher than that for telephones, but it should still be within the reach of most selection centers.

Many state and regional governmental agencies have constructed their own microwave transmission facilities for routine business. Police, highway, and road maintenance departments now use such facilities for mobile radio communication. Universities use closed-circuit television transmitted on privately owned microwave channels. With proper scheduling and added equipment, these channels can be used by local media centers for the examination of media and exchange of evaluations in regional centers prior to selection for use.

In Oklahoma the state government and industry are sharing the costs of installing a communications network for educational purposes. There will be one-way video and two-way voice communications between a classroom on the Oklahoma State University campus and consoles in industrial corporations throughout the state. A similar network was established in 1965 in Florida, based on a center for engineering education of the University of Florida near the Cape Kennedy Space Center. Networks such as this use cable or microwave transmission channels. The initial capital costs are high, but not out of reach on a statewide basis (less than $2,000,000 in Oklahoma).

Blackboard-by-wire has been demonstrated in a network by the Creative Application of Technology of Education (CATE) Center located on the Texas A & M campus. It serves fifteen schools in the Houston-Austin-Dallas triangle. Again there is a two-way audio and one-way video communication channel between the teacher and the classrooms. In this network the equipment reproduces on a television screen the information written by the teacher at a remote console.

Satellite communication facilities have the potential for providing wide-area coverage for direct communications at low cost via radio waves for several kinds of communications directly from centers to schools and homes. Space is being provided on NASA research satellites for communications experiments by the education community, and a frequency allocation will be available in the electromagnetic spectrum for educational purposes. Eventually these facilities will be available for general and widespread use.

As the facilities and capabilities of the communications industry are continuously expanded in kind and upgraded in quality, the unit cost per message per mile communicated will be reduced. While the availability of some advance facilities is limited, the technology is well developed. New channels are likely to be pre-empted in large part by major commercial users, but the education, library, and media center community that have access to such facilities should anticipate the potentials of communication technology and should prepare to adjust to the rigors of communications scheduling and protocol. The benefits will be great and highly demonstrable.

NETWORK OPERATIONS

Because of the key role of the states in setting educational goals, policies, and standards and of their funding power, communication networks designed to improve the performance of the education systems should be planned and operated on a statewide basis. Each state should, therefore, plan a thorough statewide network: a general, state-inspired educational and media selection center to set goals, help negotiate plans for and establishment of needed network lines, and lead the way towards a continuous updating of media collections throughout the state; plus regional and local subsystems. The number of subnetworks within a state should be limited and coordinated. State and federal funding for local networks should be limited to those willing to prepare for integration into a statewide system.

Networking can be introduced, however, at local and regional levels without a statewide plan and without a state media center at the hub. Unless the state is small geographically, networks are best formed by linking local centers to regional centers (county or school district centers) and thence to larger national or other regional centers with more sophisticated equipment and utilizing highly specialized staffs. The regional center would act both as an agency to expand local capabilities and to buffer and reduce the overload on the state center.

Generally, the higher in the organizational hierarchy one goes (towards the state center), the greater will be the sophistication and variety of the communications equipment. Thus a local center might use telephone lines for facsimile transmission of graphics, and communication with remote computer information files, utilizing cathode-ray tube terminals. A fuller range of transmitting facilities might be available only at a state center or the largest regional centers, for example, for the presentation of video messages and programs going out via state microwave networks and into CATV at local levels. Local centers should not be precluded from bypassing those higher in the hierarchy, but for efficiency and economy, the rights and benefits of the various agencies in the hierarchy should be carefully determined and monitored, and the priorities by which one center will serve others established.

73

Model diagrams for both a state agency-centered network and a regional agency-centered network are shown in figures 1 and 2. Models delineating paths of communication in both kinds of networks combined in an integrated national system are shown in figures 3 and 4.

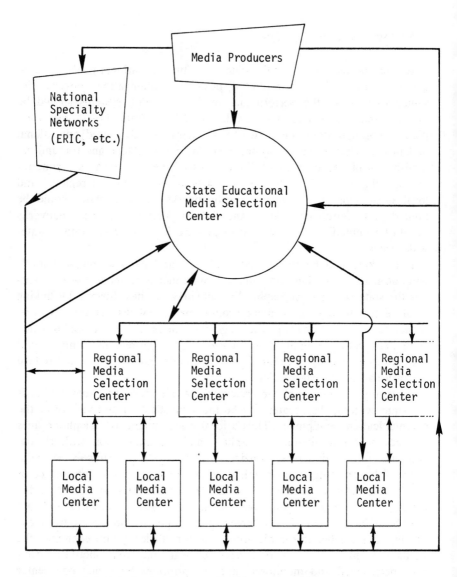

FIGURE 1. Model of a local network with a statewide center

74

STATE EDUCATIONAL MEDIA SELECTION CENTERS

The purposes of the State Educational Media Selection Center (SEMSC) are to promote and facilitate the full utilization of all media appropriate to local needs, particularly in accordance with state educational policies. It achieves these objectives chiefly through demonstration and information services, and by all available means of communication compatible with local resources. The principal users of the state educational media selection center are the centers at the regional and local levels in the state.

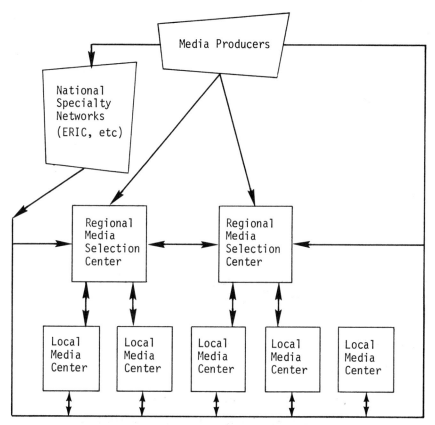

FIGURE 2. Model of a local network without a statewide center

The staff members of the SEMSC must be expert in their knowledge of the specialties of other centers, particularly within the state, and of the contents of information files in other network data bases, including many computer data bases, and the protocol for communicating with and gaining access to them. They must be able to work with several kinds of electronic keyboards, such as teletype machines, and computer terminal devices.[4]

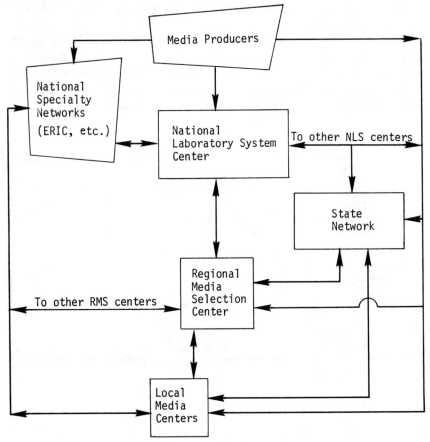

FIGURE 3. Model of a national media selection network

SEMSC Tasks

Establish and operate a state evaluation center.

Organize and supervise the operation of a coordinated statewide program for competent evaluation of media according to pertinent local concerns.

[4] This approach to information retrieval is really nothing more than is done by reference librarians who must learn the makeup and the subject heading language of many indexing and abstracting services, encyclopedias, and handbooks. In some cases it is easier to use a computer file since the software for tapping these data bases frequently includes features whereby the computer types out in natural language the precise instructions on how to take each successive step in searching the files.

76

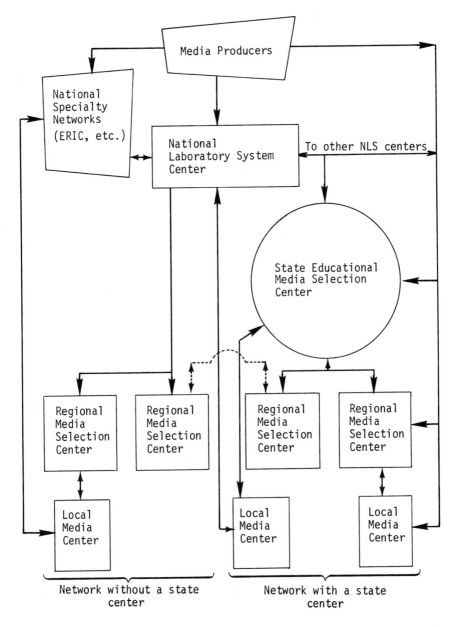

FIGURE 4. Model of a national network integrating statewide networks with and without a state center

Collect, edit, and disseminate evaluations to those responsible for selecting material. Serve chiefly the staffs of regional and local centers in the state.

Operate the principal computerized data base for storage and retrieval of information concerning media and media evaluation, using the data base provided by the national media evaluation program, augmented by state and local input.

Operate a statewide network of communications facilities. Serve as a switching center among centers within the state and for access to other state and national networks.

Perform demand and continuing reference services with regard to media evaluation and selection.

Conduct training programs in media evaluation and selection for local media center staffs, teachers, and administrators.

Monitor adherence to standards of performance of local centers.

Serve as a center in the National Laboratory System if SEMSC has a nationally recognized area of competence and expertise.

REGIONAL MEDIA SELECTION CENTERS

The difficulty, if not impossibility, of every media center in every school conducting economically and effectively its own selection center program has already been emphasized. These programs can best be carried on by readily accessible Regional Media Selection Centers (RMSC).

Every regional media selection center should aim to have the fullest possible array of communication equipment, particularly receiving equipment, to achieve virtually total access to all networks into which it can be tied. Each RMSC should be situated so that users can travel to the center, employ its resources and services, and return home in one working day. The center should not be expected to respond instantly on demand with all pertinent information in the network system. Instead, the user should try to anticipate his needs and work with the regional center through his local center prior to his visit. With sufficient time to call in information from other centers, the regional center can thus prepare for the visit in advance. The user can also be advised about how the network will most likely respond, what kinds of information and media will be available for him, and on what time schedules, at both the local and the regional center. Thus, a day's travel and work would be made most productive, and disappointing delays and voids in data gathering reduced to a minimum.

Maintains a large, up-to-date, noncirculating collection of media. Collection to be used for examination purposes by teachers, citizens, administrators, etc., to guide them in the selection of material for local acquisition and use.

Collects and maintains file of evaluations of media from local centers and users. Transmits copies of the evaluations to the state media center and to appropriate National Laboratory System Centers.

Maintains directory files of sources of information about media and of media collections elsewhere.

Offers a wide range of media services for complete examination and testing of media for local use.

Serves as a center in the National Laboratory System if RMSC has a nationally recognized area of competence and expertise in a subject area.

Maintains the most complete electronic communications capability that is available to and useful in the region.

Provides access to specialty (national) networks (e.g., ERIC central) for local centers.

Operates regional network services (e.g., film distribution network, WATS or TWX intercenter reference network).

ROLE OF THE LOCAL MEDIA SELECTION CENTER

The local educational media selection center should assist the user as much as possible with materials at hand and should help the user by linkage with the nearest regional educational media selection center. The local center will use the products of network operations, such as directories of data bases and other resources, catalogs of material available in the system, indexes and abstracts of media, and the like.

Communication facilities at local centers may currently be limited, but, in a fully operational network, they would have a telephone and teletype terminal for transmitting and receiving, and facsimile and video equipment for receiving only. To the extent that it can afford to do so, and needs dictate, the local center may provide access to national and regional networks, including those that require special electronic communications capabilities, such as remote computer terminals.

This center may also prepare evaluations of media used at the local level for inclusion in networks at higher levels in the hierarchy. This feedback, properly edited, should increase the probabilities of proper use of media in various applications and locales. Some local media centers can become large enough to serve also as regional selection centers. Those that develop a unique subject or grade-level specialty in media selection, evaluation, preparation, and use might also be designated as components in a National Laboratory System, provided, in each instance, that adequate and continuing funding is available.

The modern school media center, in providing access services to other resources, serves as a switching center in the network concept (fig. 5). Terminal equipment and accompanying software are being designed for simple manipulation, as a guarantee of widespread and general use of powerful and sophisticated information-processing tools.

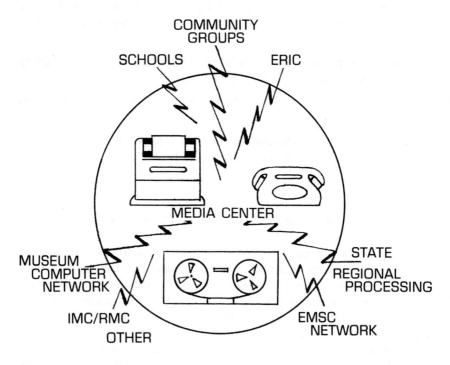

FIGURE 5. The media center as a communications and switching center

A NATIONAL NETWORK PLAN

The improvement in the performance of media centers and the dissemination of information about media through networks at regional or local levels are not entirely sufficient to assure comprehensive acquisition, evaluation, selection, and local application of all media for all subjects. Total access to such a vast inventory of evaluative information requires a network with national components.

Accordingly, the Executive and Advisory Committees of the National Book Committee's EMSC Program propose that a network of centers—a National Laboratory System (NLS)—be established: to collect media under the direction of a controlled plan to cover all media, all subjects, and all levels of applicability of the media; to provide complete descriptive bibliography for the media; to prepare evaluations of the media; to collect evaluations made by other recognized authorities under identifiable circumstances; and to provide nationwide access to information useful in the selection process at local levels. (Models of such a network are shown in figures 3 and 4.)

Briefly, the national network can be described as follows. National centers, each assigned to a subject (or subjects) and perhaps a grade level, acquire from publishers and other creators and producers of media, all of the media likely to be of value to education (as previously defined). These centers, designated National Laboratory System Centers (NLSC), are responsible for complete cataloging of those media not already cataloged professionally elsewhere, for their evaluation, at least in general terms, and for dissemination of information about the media continuously and on demand.

The principal customers of the services of the NLS are state and regional media selection centers and media specialists, faculty, and concerned individuals at local media centers at the building or district level in school systems or in the community at large. The regional selection centers are responsible for acquiring for local inspection and selection all of the media potentially appropriate to local needs, using information obtained from the NLSC components of the network as well as locally derived information. Ultimately, the goal is to increase the holdings of useful media in the local media centers where it is most convenient for use with students, librarians, and other segments of the user population.

Linkages are provided at all levels of this national network with other national information networks, such as the Educational Research Information Centers (ERIC),[5] Special Education for the Deaf, the Instructional

[5] ERIC Headquarters, U.S. Office of Education, 400 Maryland Avenue, S.W., Washington, D.C. 20202.

Materials Center/Regional Media Centers (IMC/RMC) Network,[6] and centers for the handicapped. The output of these other networks is useful at the national level to help identify the range of media and services appropriate to selection process, and at the regional and local levels to identify media applicable to specific tasks and problems in the schools and communities. Regional and local media centers also fit into, or at least tap, state and other regional networks operating to provide access to media and information about them.

The communication and information-processing tasks implied by this network configuration are large. It should be anticipated, therefore, that the National Laboratory System Centers and the regional media selection centers will require highly trained professional staffs involved both in the substance of the subjects and in information science, and a wide array of sophisticated communication components.

While there may be a number of paths from node to node in the network, the best search strategy will follow certain paths more often than others. For example, local centers may go more frequently to the state network through the regional media selection center where their requests are searched against local regional holdings before transfer to the state library. Nothing should prevent the local center from connecting with the state network directly from time to time, however, if it has the terminal equipment, can pay the communication costs, and can reasonably anticipate that a regional center cannot serve its need.

NATIONAL LABORATORY SYSTEM CENTERS

The purposes of the National Laboratory System are to acquire exhaustive collections of media; to provide complete descriptive cataloging of the media, including sufficient subject analysis to allow at least gross selection by this approach; to conduct as complete evaluations of the media as is possible at a national level; to coordinate and collect evaluations made elsewhere; and to offer information dissemination and media reference services of various kinds based on these collections and evaluations.

These centers should, if possible, be located in existing centers, agencies, or institutions where the subject and the media are already of concern and where specialists in the evaluation and use of the media for that subject would most likely be available. Some existing centers could be induced to take on this added responsibility where they have subject discipline expertise. They should, of course, be compensated for the added burden they

[6] 1499 Jefferson Davis Highway, Suite 928, Arlington, Va. 22202.

would assume on behalf of users in the national network who are not their primary responsibility.[7]

NLSC TASKS

Collect all media possible in their assigned subjects and grade levels.

Catalog all the media.

Make at least general evaluations of the media.

Offer various information services based on the media and related data:

Publish a regular catalog with suitable indexes and annotations; these might be in print or in other formats.

Publish occasional and continuing catalogs of media and evaluative information in subjects of special national interest.

Prepare special catalogs according to local specifications as might be requested by local groups, centers, etc.

Offer demand information services to answer questions about media in their subject areas as they occur. This service should ultimately be computer based, with online access from local sources.

Offer seminars and workshops on a national basis for training in media evaluation, selection, and use.

Maintain demonstration laboratories for the use of media that might be especially useful in their assigned fields.

From cumulative experience, recommended guidelines and standards for improving media.

These national centers should serve chiefly other centers in the system. Direct approach by individuals should be discouraged in order to channel the user into his closest local and regional centers where his needs can be assessed, a network search strategy worked out, and the full potential of the available resources from many places mobilized with an economy of effort on the part of both the users and the centers in the system.

---

[7] The Farmington Plan was designed to increase the amount of material held in research libraries in the United States with minimum duplication, and the ERIC system works this way, although the libraries in the Farmington plan bore all of the costs of their participation.

83

MANAGEMENT OF MEDIA INFORMATION
IN A NATIONAL NETWORK

The achievement of the goals of the national network will be chiefly a function of communication. Regardless of the success the National Laboratory System Center and the state and regional centers have in acquiring and cataloging media, they will not be able to serve the selection process in local media centers unless they can package and disseminate the information they have gathered and generated, in a style and with the timeliness required to suit local selection tasks.

The design of data files, the systems to update, probe, and purge them, and the packages for communication along various channels are tasks of major proportions, subject to influences that will have to be identified in the next phase of the EMSC Program. Again, however, there are models of similar operations in other networks that suggest appropriate techniques and systems components in general.

Most logically, the categories of information to be generated, stored, packaged, and disseminated in an educational media selection network will be:

> *Cataloging information*, including a complete and standard description of each item, and subject descriptors for additional processing control

> *Content information*, including informative abstracts and complete evaluations from various sources, in the style and depth determined elsewhere in this program to be essential to the selection process.

The cataloging and content information is generated principally by the National Laboratory System Centers and the state centers, although provision should be made for NLS Centers to accept standard information from other sources (e.g., Machine-Readable Cataloging Data [MARC] from the Library of Congress, when available). The NLS Centers will operate the principal specialized storage, retrieval, and dissemination files for the network.

Evaluative information will come from several sources. Specialists on the NLSC and state center staffs will provide initial evaluation for much of the media. Provision should be made to accept evaluations from the field as the media are used. Manuals or guides to evaluation techniques, system standards and criteria, and standard reporting forms should be prepared to facilitate field reporting. The system should record the circumstances and location of the field evaluations, and perhaps the name of the evaluating

84

person, group, or agency. This information will itself be valuable in the selection process. All evaluation information should be reviewed by specialists in the NLS and state centers before entry into the files, which will grow into useful "clusters" of evaluations.

The volume of data thus collected will be massive, but it will be most tractable and responsive to computer processing. It is most desirable, therefore, that at least the cataloging and content information be processed into machine-readable form so that the computer may be used to store, retrieve, format, update, and purge. Also, in this format the records can more readily be used to generate signals for electronic input devices in communication systems.

To take full advantage of computer operations, including communication among computers in various centers, and to do so economically, a high degree of compatability will be required in NLSC operations. If each center is left to organize and operate its own computer facilities, the system should at least adopt a standard record format for the communication of machine-readable files among them. The MARC formats for various forms of media as developed by the Library of Congress are recommended. Similar formats can be developed by the NLS Centers for those forms of media not yet handled by the Library of Congress. It would be essential for the entire system also to use the same style of subject analysis and forms of subject entry. Authority lists would need to be cooperatively compiled and shared.

It would be desirable if one computer and concomitant software could be used for cataloging control for the entire system of NLS Centers. The centers could send information in various ways for entry into the central file, and the file could be accessed electronically (e.g., by telephone) from remote sites, with one set of instructions and one protocol system for the entire spectrum of media and for all centers. This proposal suggests a high degree of sophistication and control that might well be too costly, both to develop and to use. But the feasibility of the idea should be explored.

Experience gained by persons already engaged in the design and implementation of computer-supported systems, such as the Automated Instructional Materials Handling System (AIMS) for use in the Los Angeles Unified School District and other large urban districts, should be extremely valuable.

The principal output of the NLS and state centers will be catalog listings of media on a regular and frequent basis, containing standard cataloging information, brief annotations, and abstracted evaluations (perhaps in the fashion of the H. W. Wilson Company's *Book Review Digest*). In some cases the catalogs will contain suitable indexes, cumulated frequently as required. Each NLS and state center may issue its own catalog, or entries from all centers may be pooled for issuance by a central source. Again,

85

careful study will be required to determine the best course of action. If separate catalogs are issued, it would be desirable for them to utilize the same style of presentation, format, and indexing to facilitate local use. The catalogs will be the principle source of information for regional media selection centers in their identification of media for potential selection. The evaluative information supplied with the catalogs should be styled to be sufficiently informative to allow selection of media for the regional media selection centers without further reference to the full text of evaluations. If, however, full text of evaluations is likely to be required very frequently at the regional level, microfiche publication of the evaluation sheets is recommended, perhaps on a selective subscription basis.

Once the catalogs are produced, information in the files will be available for special searches tailored to customer demand and for the production of additional catalogs on special aspects of various topics as deemed appropriate and marketable. At this point the various files from all NLS Centers might be merged by a central or commercial agency to create catalogs and perform subject searches that cut across the lines of a number of NLSC interests.

There is still one more advantage to machine-readable data bases important to the goals of the EMSC Program. These files can be sold in machine-readable form for local use wherever computers are available.

Thus a well-financed media center can operate its own computerized information services for local users with the same power of the large NLS Centers. The evaluative information will most likely be lengthy and voluminous. Although it might be converted to machine-readable format to generate printed catalogs, it might not be economical to store format for subsequent demand searching services. This characteristic of the network system must be carefully researched before sound decisions can be made. The Science Information Exchange (SIE) operates a combination computer-index and hardcopy data file that might be emulated by the EMSC Program. In this configuration, evaluative information would be supplied to the file operators in the NLS and state centers on standard forms. Searches to identify media according to user specifications would be made in the computer-index files. Evaluation sheets for media items identified in the searches would be retrieved by hand from the evaluation files, photocopied or microfilmed, and sent to the customer. SIE conducts as many as 60,000 searches a year in a file of about 100,000 items in this fashion.

CONCLUSIONS

Networking of educational media selection centers is a practical, organic development, growing upward from those centers reflecting and serving local needs. The engineering of a plan of this magnitude is a major under-taking. A number of collateral questions and conditions would, naturally, have to be resolved: for example, the codification of compatible criteria and procedures for the evaluation process. Federal funding would have to be assured, and a coordinating agency appointed or created to supply the necessary impetus. The relationships of the proposed National Laboratory System to the regional structure and laboratories of the U.S. Office of Education, to the National Institute of Education, and to the recommended institutes of educational technology, would, of course, have to be explored with care.

As an integral part of Phase III of the Educational Media Selection Center Program, therefore, a special task force or team should be organized to survey the feasibility of establishing an EMSC network, with national as well as local, regional, and state nodes or components. Concurrently, as model/demonstration centers at different levels are developed, they should be equipped with, at least, the basic communications devices which will ultimately link them to the proposed national network.

10

Summary and Conclusions

This Guide presents a comprehensive definition of the scope, objectives and programs of educational media selection centers, innovative resources for improving and extending the use of media in a variety of educational and community settings. It recognizes distinctions between the concepts and functions of the EMSC Program and school libraries and instructional media centers, yet stresses the essential links between and among all kinds of service-oriented resource people and collections.

An EMSC program has two major functions: the collection and evaluation of a comprehensive range of educational media, and the continuous education, primarily inservice, of its clientele in the effective selection and use of media. The client groups of an EMSC program include, of course, classroom teachers and media specialists in formal public and private school systems. However, an essential EMSC program function is to reach those who are engaged in every kind of organized instructional effort including, for example, social and civic groups, antipoverty agencies, child day-care personnel, community and neighborhood information centers, and other similar personnel.

As EMSC programs begin to function on a more comprehensive basis, this external orientation will make possible an effective articulation with the many emerging activities in nontraditional education. Independent study directed towards student-selected goals, open-classroom activities, compensatory education needs at the junior college level created by open-enrollment policies, and the increasing array of special reading and literacy programs are among the developments with increasing implications for EMSC programs of resources and services. A number of different auspices under which EMSC programs might be operated have been suggested in preceding chapters. In every case this reaching-out to all the appropriate elements of the educational community is stressed.

The Guide describes illustrative client groups, various possible organizational structures, and lines of responsibility and authority for the successful operation of EMSC programs. It offers both a conceptual basis and practical suggestions for the creation or extension of a full EMSC program. Those responsible for educational planning and administration will find that a well-conceived and operated EMSC program will permit the fullest possible application of media to instructional experiences with efficiency and economy. The Guide stresses the point: the most practical place to begin an EMSC program is at the local level.

The communications role of EMSC programs is given careful attention. As evaluations become available, the Guide recommends that the information be selectively disseminated to client groups and individuals using interest profiles maintained under the center program. These targeted communications would then be supplemented by a variety of more general bulletin listings, including data on subject and grade- or age-level research. Program review and evaluation are also treated as essential components of the EMSC program.

The conclusions contained in the Guide are presented neither as explicit nor as comprehensive recommendations. Rather, the Guide itself is a validation of the EMSC program concept with specific attention to organization, administration programs, collections, facilities and budgets. With respect to the interaction among different EMSC programs, the Guide returns to the more general and conceptual level. The consensus of contributors is clearly that synergistic relationships will emerge as more independent EMSC programs come into existence. Various networking patterns and possible applications of communications technology are explored, but more operational experience is required before the most feasible and desirable structures can be designed. The Guide does make clear, however, that such networking is a practical, organic development which will, indeed must, emerge from the collateral efforts of independent EMSC programs.

A systematic and controlled method of securing more operational experience, including networking, is referred to in the Guide as Phase III of the EMSC Program. This third phase envisions a model, or a pilot, system of local, district, and regional programs situated in different administrative and geographic locations with a headquarters responsible for communications and program review. If only one model is selected, a state model might be the most desirable. In order to build on existing strengths, most of the pilot components would be programs already operating at a substantial level of effectiveness. Such a demonstration effort should, however, make some provision for creating an EMSC program component where the need and interest are strong but where no such services are available at the inception of the model phase. The choices of model center programs should yield an optimum mix to test and evaluate different bases for center operation.

Appendix 1: Advisers

EMSC EXECUTIVE ADVISORY COUNCIL MEMBERS
(1968–1970)

MASON W. GROSS, *Chairman*
Rutgers
The State University of New Jersey

JOHN ROWELL
EMSC Project Director
School of Library Science
Case Western Reserve University

M. ANN HEIDBREDER
EMSC Project Coordinator
National Book Committee, Inc.

ELENORA ALEXANDER
Houston Independent School District

ARTHUR BRODY
Bro-Dart Industries

O. L. DAVIS, JR.
University of Texas at Austin

ROBERT C. GERLETTI
Los Angeles County Schools

ALVIN J. GOLDWYN
Case Western Reserve University

FRANCES HENNE
Columbia University

MARY FRANCES K. JOHNSON
University of North Carolina at
Greensboro

CARL L. MARBURGER
New Jersey State Department of
Education

MOST REVEREND JOHN B. MCDOWELL
Diocese of Pittsburgh

A. EDWARD MILLER
The World Publishing Company

FRANKLIN PATTERSON
Hampshire College

HAROLD W. TUCKER
Queens Borough Public Library

THEODORE WALLER
Grolier Educational Corporation

91

ADVISORY COMMITTEE

ANDREW J. MITCHELL
Department of Elementary School
Principals

HELEN HUUS
International Reading Association

WILLIAM G. HARLEY
National Association of
Educational Broadcasters

CARY POTTER
National Association of
Independent Schools

CURTIS JOHNSON
National Association of Secondary
School Principals

JOHN C. ELLINGSON
National Audio-Visual
Association, Inc.

REVEREND C. ALBERT KOOB
The National Catholic Educational
Association

GERALD E. SROUFE
National Committee for the
Support of the Public Schools

ELIZABETH HENDRYSON
National Congress of Parents
and Teachers

RALPH W. CORDIER
National Council for the
Social Studies

WILLIAM A. JENKINS
National Council of Teachers of
English

JULIUS H. HLAVATY
The National Council of Teachers of
Mathematics

NELL WHITE
National Education Association

EDWIN G. COHEN
National Instructional Television
Center

GEORGIANA HARDY
National School Boards Association

ELIZABETH A. SIMENDINGER
National Science Teachers Association

ROBERT T. FILEP
National Society for Programmed
Instruction

GORDON I. SWANSON
Rural Education Association

EXECUTIVE COMMITTEE OF THE EMSC
ADVISORY COMMITTEE
(1971–   )

MASON W. GROSS, *Chairman*
Formerly President
Rutgers, The State University
of New Jersey

FRANCES HENNE, *Vice Chairman*
School of Library Service
Columbia University

CORA PAUL BOMAR
EMSC Program Director
School of Education
The University of North Carolina
at Greensboro

CAROL A. NEMEYER
EMSC Program Coordinator
National Book Committee

93

ARTHUR BRODY, President
Bro-Dart Publishing Company

ALEXANDER FRAZIER
College of Education
The Ohio State University

MARY V. GAVER, Director
Library Consulting Services
Bro-Dart Publishing Company

ROBERT C. GERLETTI, Director
Division of Educational Media
Los Angeles County Schools

M. ANN HEIDBREDER
Director of Library Services
Harcourt Brace Jovanovich, Inc.

MONTERIA HIGHTOWER
Director of Institutional Libraries
Maryland State Department of
Education

MARY FRANCES K. JOHNSON
School of Education
The University of North Carolina at
Greensboro

DOROTHY M. MCGEOCH
Department of Clinical Experiences
New York State University at
Potsdam

A. EDWARD MILLER, President
Downe Publishing, Inc.

FRANKLIN PATTERSON, President
Hampshire College

JOHN ROWELL
School of Library Science
Case Western Reserve University

HAROLD W. TUCKER, Director
Queens Borough Public Library

THEODORE WALLER, President
Grolier Educational Corporation

Appendix 2: Budget for a State-Level Examination Center

CENTER — ANNUAL EXPENSES (1972–73)

Rental — includes utilities and custodial services	$12,540.00
Salaries — 1 professional	
1 clerk-steno I	19,188.00
(The salary range for professionals on this level is $12,075–$15,387 depending on years of service.)	
(The salary range for clerk-steno I is $4,551–$5,803 depending on years of service.)	
Postage (annual)	600.00
Telephone (annual)	2,000.00
Travel ($125.00 monthly average)	1,500.00
Business supplies (paper, envelopes, file folders, mail boxes, etc.)	325.00
To maintain and add to collection, print and nonprint	30,000.00
To maintain equipment (bulbs, repairs, etc.)	250.00
To add to equipment	500.00
To add to furniture (shelving, chairs, etc.)	500.00

INITIAL INSTALLATION (1966)

Books	$25,000.00
Shelving — 60 sections double-faced	2,400.00
Furniture	
3 desks	600.00
1 sofa	200.00
2 large chairs	200.00
4 armchairs	100.00
40 folding chairs	120.00
metal bookcase	75.00
card catalog	750.00
3 filing cases	300.00
4 metal tables	225.00
1 folding table	75.00
1 double file table	125.00
2 study tables	80.00
1 book truck	80.00
1 AV truck	50.00

3 typewriters (1 electric)	$ 650.00
1 storage cabinet	150.00
1 dictionary/atlas stand	229.00

Postage meter (rented)
1 coat rack
2 clothes trees
bulletin board
step stool
desk lamps $ 500.00
waste baskets
book supports
book display racks
miscellaneous business supplies

AV EQUIPMENT

16mm projector
8mm filmloop projector
8mm filmloop projector (sound)
1   reel-to-reel tape recorder
6   cassette tape recorders
1   phonograph
6   hand viewers
1   screen
1   small table screen $ 5,000.00
1   filmstrip and cassette previewer
1   filmstrip and record previewer
1   portable projector table
1   overhead projector
1   camera (35mm)
1   autoload fs projector
1   ampli-vox diplomat amplifier

ON LOAN FROM MANUFACTURERS

carrels
picture book tables
chairs
benches, stools
portable (folding) carrels
reader-printer
microfilm readers
projectors
cassette players

NOTE: Although the above figures represent actual costs, they should be interpreted as an example of one state at a particular time. The figures are suggestive, not conclusive. The program described was funded by ESEA Title II, although in several previous years some state funds were used to maintain the center's program.

The initial collection of nonprint materials and most of the necessary hardware were provided by manufacturers. The hardware collection continues to be developed, primarily through acquisition. Since 1971/72 nonprint materials have been purchased. In 1973 Mrs. Elizabeth P. Hoffman, Chief, Division of School Libraries and Coordinator of ESEA Title II and Textbook Section, Act 195, reported that the cost of evaluating media for all children in the state of Pennsylvania is 88 cents per pupil. This figure is derived by dividing the total cost of the three centers in operation by the number of children served.

Selected Bibliography

"AASL Urges Organized and Wise Use of Trade Book Examination Centers." *Library Journal* 88: 1308–9 (March 15, 1963).

American Association of School Libraries, Supervisors Section. *Supervision of School Library Media Programs.* Chicago: American Library Assn., 1971.

American Library Association and National Educational Association. *Standards for School Media Programs.* Chicago: American Library Assn.; Washington, D.C.: National Education Assn., 1969.

"Annotated Bibliography on the Cost of Education." *Audiovisual Instruction,* Nov. 1971, p.25–28.

Association for Educational Communications and Technology. *Standards for Cataloging Nonprint Materials.* rev. ed. Washington, D.C.: The Association, 1971.

Barron, Robert E., comp. "Publications in Curriculum and Media." *The Bookmark* 30, no.2: 60–69 (Nov. 1970).

Becker, Joseph, and Wallace C. Olsen. "Information Networks." In *Annual Review of Information Science and Technology,* ed. by Carlos Cuadra. Chicago: Encyclopaedia Britannica, 1968.

Blum, Eleanor. *Basic Books in the Mass Media.* Urbana: University of Illinois Pr., 1971.

Brickell, Henry M. "Implementing Educational Change." *School Libraries,* Summer 1970, p.17–23.

Brown, James W., Kenneth D. Norberg, and Sara K. Srygley. *Administering Educational Media.* New York: McGraw-Hill, 1972.

Burns, Judith. "The Joint Standards: Media or Mediocrity?" *Educational Technology* 11, no.9: 53–56 (Sept. 1971).

Clapp, Verner W. "The Greatest Invention since the Title-Page? Autobiography from Incipit to Cataloging-in-Publication." *Wilson Library Bulletin* 46, no.4: 348–59 (Dec. 1971).

————. "Public Libraries and the Network Idea," *Library Journal* 95: 121–24 (Jan. 15, 1970).

Coyne, Walter. "Education's Rising Star," *American Education* 8, no.9: 16–24 (Nov. 1972).

Erickson, Carlton W. H. *Administering Instructional Media.* New York: Macmillan, 1968.

Friedman, Burton Dean. "Program-Oriented Information: A Management Systems Complex for State Education Agencies. Part 1: Analysis and Proposals." Baltimore, Md.: State Dept. of Education, 1961.

Gaver, Mary Virginia. *Background Reading in Building Media Collections.* vols. 1 and 2. Metuchen, N.J.: Scarecrow, 1969.

Geller, Evelyn. "A Media Troika And MARC," *School Library Journal,* Jan. 1972, p.25–29.

Harris, Ben. *In-Service Education: A Guide to Better Practice.* Englewood Cliffs, N.J.: Prentice-Hall, 1969.

Hartley, Harry J. *Educational Planning-Programing-Budgeting: A Systems Approach.* Englewood Cliffs, N.J.: Prentice-Hall, 1968.

Henne, Frances. "Preconditional Factors Affecting the Reading of Young People." Ph.D. dissertation, University of Chicago, 1949.

————. "Standards for School Library Services at the District Level." *Library Trends* 16: 502–11 (April 1968).

Hensel, Evelyn, and Peter D. Veillette. *Purchasing Library Materials in Public and School Libraries.* Chicago: American Library Assn., 1969.

Lewis, Philip, ed. "New Dimensions in Educational Technology for Multi-Media Centers." *Library Trends* 19, no.4 (April 1971).

Lohrer, Alice. "The Identification and Role of School Libraries that Function as Instructional Materials Centers and Implications for Library Education in the United States." Urbana: University of Illinois, Graduate School of Library Science, 1970.

McCauley, Elfreda. "Computers in School Libraries." *School Libraries* 20: 28–32 (Winter 1971).

McJenkin, Virginia. "School System Programs of In-Service Education on the School Library as a Materials Center." In *The School Library as a Materials Center,* ed. by Mary Helen Mahar. Washington, D.C.: Govt. Printing Office, 1963 (U.S. Office of Education Publication no.OE–15042).

Meierhenry, W. C. *Media Competencies for Teachers*: A Project to Identify Competencies Needed by Teachers in the Use of the Newer Media and Various Approaches to Achieving Them. Lincoln: University of Nebraska, 1966 (U.S. Office of Education Contract no.ED–012–713).

Melcher, Daniel. *Melcher on Acquisition.* Chicago: American Library Assn., 1971.

Merritt, LeRoy Charles. *Book Selection and Intellectual Freedom.* New York: Wilson, 1970.

Mersky, Roy M. "Library Laws," *Encyclopedia Americana.*

Miller, Richard I. *Selecting New Aids to Teaching.* Washington, D.C.: Assn. for Supervision and Curriculum Development, 1971.

National Academy of Science, Information Systems Panel, Computer Science and Engineering Board. *Libraries and Information Technology: A National Systems Challenge.* Washington, D.C.: The Academy, 1972.

New York Educational Communication Association and Division of Educational Communications, State Education Department, *New York State Educational Communication Standards.* Melville, N.Y.: The Department, 1970.

Pennsylvania Learning Resources Association. *Guidelines for Instructional Media Services Programs.* West Chester, Pa.: Service Project and Area Research Center, 1970.

Perlman, Stephen B. *Legal Aspects of Selected Issues in Telecommunications.* Montvale, N.J.: AFIPS Pr., 1970.

Rowell, John, and M. Ann Heidbreder. *Educational Media Selection Centers.* Chicago: American Library Assn., 1971.

Rufsvold, Margaret I., and Carolyn Guss. *Guides to Educational Media.* 3rd ed. Chicago: American Library Assn., 1971.

School Library Manpower Project. *Occupational Definitions for School Library Media Personnel.* Chicago: American Library Assn., 1971.

Shaughnessy, Thomas. "The Influence of Distance and Travel Time on Central Library Use." Ph.D. dissertation, Rutgers, The State University, 1970.

Stone, Elizabeth W. "Continuing Education: Avenue to Adventure." *School Libraries.* 18: 37–46 (Summer 1969).

Swanker, Esther, and M. Ann Heidbreder. "Project: A Book Examination Center." *Library Journal* 91, no.4: 1031–32 (Feb. 1966).

Tanzman, Jack. "A Study to Explore the Role and Feasibility of a Regional Educational Communications Center." Plainview, Tex.: Plainview-Old Bethpage Public Schools, 1964 (U.S. Office of Education Contract no.OE–3–16–042).

Tickton, Sidney G., ed. *To Improve Learning: An Evaluation of Instructional Technology.* 2 vols. New York: Bowker, 1971.

Vann, Sarah K. *Southeastern Pennsylvania Processing Center Feasibility Study: Final Report.* (Harrisburg, Pa.: Pennsylvania State Library, Dept. of Public Instruction, 1967.)

Weihs, Jean Riddle, Shirley Lewis, and Janet Macdonald. *Non-Book Materials: The Organization of Integrated Collections.* Prepared in consultation with the CLA/ALA/AECT/EMAC/CAML Advisory Committee on the Cataloging of Nonbook Materials. 1st ed. Ottawa: Canadian Library Assn., 1973; distr. in U.S. by American Library Assn., Chicago.

Wheeler, Joseph L., and Herbert Goldhor. *Practical Administration of Public Libraries.* New York: Harper & Row, 1962.

————. "Top Priority for Cataloging-in-Source." *Library Journal* 94, no.16: 3007–13 (Sept. 15, 1969).

Willis, Charles L. "Emerging Patterns of School District Organization with Implications for School Library Service." *Library Trends.* 16: 429–34 (April 1968).